P9-CQM-672

Ex Líbrís

Randy Manning

GARDENING
IN TIME

PLANNING FUTURE GROWTH AND FLOWERING

GARDENING IN TIME

CAROLINE BOISSET

AMERICAN EDITOR: FAYAL GREENE

PRENTICE
HALL
PRESS

NEW YORK • LONDON • TORONTO • SYDNEY • TOKYO • SINGAPORE

To my dear husband, John Carter

PRENTICE HALL PRESS
15 Columbus Circle
New York, NY 10023

Copyright © Mitchell Beazley Publishers 1990
Text copyright © Caroline Boisset 1990
Artwork copyright © Mitchell Beazley Publishers 1990

All rights reserved, including the right of reproduction
in whole or in part in any form.

Originally published in Great Britain.

PRENTICE HALL PRESS and colophons are
registered trademarks of Simon & Schuster, Inc.

Library of Congress Catalog Card Number: 89-043587

ISBN 0-13-346230-7

Edited and designed by
Mitchell Beazley International Ltd,
Artists House, 14-15 Manette Street, London W1V 5LB

Senior Art Editor: Eljay Crompton
Assistant Art Editor: Jane Ryan
Editorial Assistant: Jaspal Kharay
Color Artwork: Fiona Bell Currie
                       Liz Pepperell
Production: Ted Timberlake

Executive Editor: Robert Saxton

Typeset in Helvetica Light by Litho Link Ltd,
Welshpool, Powys, Wales
Color reproduction by Scantrans Pte, Singapore
Manufactured by Graficas Estella, S.A., Navarra, Spain

10   9   8   7   6   5   4   3   2   1

First Prentice Hall Press Edition

CONTENTS

INTRODUCTION

One of the greatest pleasures in gardening is to experience the continual changes that take place as the seasons and the years progress. *Gardening in Time* is a book about how to manage these changes in order to make of the garden a perpetually unfolding composition — like an endless piece of music. To achieve this is a considerable challenge, because you will need to predict how fast plants grow, and how they will look (individually and together) in all stages of their growth and throughout the seasons, as well as how to maintain them correctly. All this, within the possibilities allowed by soil conditions and climate, is the essence of garden planning, and can occupy many stimulating hours outside the garden.

To begin with, it is important to understand the plants. How much water, light, heat and nutrition will each one require, and when? Will growth be rapid and eventually difficult to keep in check, or will it be frustratingly slow? Growth is the topic of the first major section of this book, and I hope that the pages that chart graphically the growth rates of selected plants will do much to clarify understanding. I have not been put off by the possibility that the performance of individual specimens may not precisely follow the norm: the general pattern of expectation is clear enough, despite any variations accounted for by the particular conditions in which a plant grows.

Most of those who read this book will probably have relatively small gardens, and this is a point I have tried to bear constantly in mind. However, the principles I outline and the suggestions I make apply to gardens of all sizes.

Each site has its own microclimate and topography, and it is always best to work with these factors, not against them. In looking at how the time dimension needs to be related to the specifics of the site ("Time

and Place"), I have drawn on the experience of other gardeners, particularly in focusing on a shady, sunny, dry and damp garden, with photographs of each as they change through the year. Plants derive originally from a wide range of natural habitats around the world, from the forests of northern Europe to the cool, high-altitude region of the Himalayas. If you learn which plants come from which habitats, you will more readily be able to select a plant that is suitable for a particular site in your garden.

Mainly, this book is designed to assist those whose aim is the establishment of a garden that will give sustained pleasure in maturity — whether starting from a virgin site or from an inherited garden. However, I know from experience how important it is to make a garden interesting in the short term, before the longer-term plan is fulfilled. Hence the section in this book entitled "Timely Solutions", which looks at ways to obtain rapid results.

The success of a garden usually depends on carefully synchronized effects throughout the year. In "Season by Season" I look at various strategies for making time an ally in the creation of beautiful harmonies and contrasts — especially of flowers and foliage, but not forgetting fruit and bark, which play a key role outside the growing season. I include some specific plans for borders that reach a climax in spring, summer and autumn, with suggestions to extend the season and fill the gaps in the first year of growth.

My hope is that *Gardening in Time* will be valued by both novice and experienced gardeners, not only for the practical information it brings together, but for its ideas and suggestions. Gardening is an adventure, offering limitless scope for change. If you try something new and it fails to please, never mind: there is always next year.

Caroline Boisset

ACKNOWLEDGMENTS

I would like to express my sincere gratitude to the many people who have freely given their knowledge, skills and support during the preparation of this book. I particularly mention Bob Saxton and Eljay Crompton, at Mitchell Beazley, and David Joyce.

For the outstanding series of photographs I have to thank the hard work and imagination of Paul Barker, Andrew Lawson and Jerry Harpur; for the true and artistic interpretation of my sometimes sketchy plans and ideas, Fiona Bell Currie and Liz Pepperell.

Finally, my warmest thanks to the many creators and owners of beautiful gardens who also have patiently and kindly endured the repeated visits of our photographers and answered my endless questions: Beth Chatto, Mrs Sybil Spencer, Mrs Eileen Marshall, Mrs Gill Richardson, Mrs Gwen Beaumont and Mrs Iris Pugh.

Given the right growing conditions, herbaceous plants and bulbs will fill a bed in two or three years. Here, a spring composition in a sunny part of the garden is dominated by the dark tulip 'Queen of the Night', which stands out clearly against the lime-yellow bracts of *Euphorbia polychroma* and the golden yellow flowers of the double buttercup (*Ranunculus acris* 'Flore Pleno'). As these plants fade, poppies and perennial wallflowers will take over the limelight. A variegated holly – a plant that takes many years to reach maturity – creates an all-year background to this well-composed group of plants.

GROWTH AND CONTROL

One of the keys to creating a successful garden is choosing the right plants for the right place in a way that takes fully into account what can be expected of each plant throughout its lifespan. The right choice, therefore, is not simply a matter of selecting for color or seasonal interest. You need to know what growing conditions a plant requires to develop to healthy maturity and how long it will take to reach its optimum size. The biological optimum is not necessarily when a plant will look its mature best, so you also need to know when a plant will reach its esthetic optimum. With this information you can plan both for the long term, including eventual replacement, and for the short term – for example, the need for some supplementary planting initially.

To grow properly, all plants have certain basic requirements, and of these water is probably the most important. It is necessary for the germination of seeds and during the growing season, but it will be detrimental to a plant during its resting period. In the temperate world this is normally the winter, although many plants, such as bulbs, rest during the summer and start growing in the autumn.

Making sure that a plant has sufficient water while actively growing will help it reach its mature potential. The volume of water required varies greatly from plant to plant: pelargoniums, for example, require much less water to survive than petunias. However, generally speaking, young and small plants, annuals and herbaceous species, or pot-grown plants, will be most susceptible to water loss, and wilting will occur quite quickly if the available water drops below a certain level. Once wilted, they will recover quickly if given water without delay, but the point is soon reached when they cannot be revived. With woody species the effect of water loss is slower and less visible. They are larger and have deeper roots and more resources to draw on, but they will nevertheless be affected.

Of course, it is not necessarily possible to water plants in the open ground throughout the season. For certain fruit and vegetables, for example, there is an optimum time at which they should be watered to obtain the maximum yield. This is most often just after the crop has formed but before it ripens. Too much water at a late stage produces fruit and vegetables that are tasteless.

As the season draws to an end, growth must slow down to prepare the plant for the period of rest. It is often not low temperatures but the high water content of a plant that causes it to rot and die during its inactive phase. In their natural environment

PRINCIPLES OF GROWTH

The sequence on the opposite page shows stages from late winter to autumn in the growth of bulbs, perennials and roses sited in a partly shady border.

Top left: Late winter. Although many herbaceous and bulbous plants have started into growth, the only plant in flower is a Christmas rose (*Helleborus niger*). The vigorous climbing rose, *R. heleni*, against the brick wall has a well-established frame of spreading branches that have had their annual pruning.

Top right: Late spring. The young foliage is well developed. The risk of competition from weeds is reduced by dense planting of herbaceous plants, including *Hosta sieboldiana* 'Elegans', *H.* 'Frances Williams', geraniums (including *G. macrorrhizum*), and a brunnera (*B. macrophylla*) displaying its blue flowers.

Bottom left: By mid-summer most plants have reached their mature height. Both roses (*R. heleni* and *R. glauca*) have finished flowering, but the astrantia is a sea of creamy and rosy white flowers emphasized by the blue of the chicory.

Bottom right: In autumn the roses are covered in hips, the astrantia seed heads are ripening and the hosta leaves are turning yellow before the foliage begins to wilt and die as the days grow shorter and temperatures drop.

small alpines are protected from wet during the winter by a layer of snow. In wet lowland conditions, covering them with a sheet of glass through winter will help to keep them dry and increase their chances of survival.

The physical composition of the soil will play a vital role in regulating the availability of water and therefore affects the growth of plants. If you want to grow a wide range of plants in areas where rainfall is high during the growing season, it is best to have a freely draining soil. Where dry periods are prevalent, a moisture-retentive soil will be more suitable. Soils with fine particles, such as clay and sand, drain most freely, while soils with large particles, such as loam, are more moisture-retentive.

Nutrients necessary to the wellbeing of plants are present in the soil as chemical compounds. They are transmitted to the plants in water and must therefore be available in a water-soluble form. The three main nutrients are nitrogen, phosphorus and potassium (known as NPK) and if these are not available in sufficient quantities growth will be very slow. Standard chemical fertilizers contain these three elements in varying proportions. If fertilizers are applied at the beginning of the growing season, plants can make plenty of growth early on and have time to ripen before the rest period. Magnesium is another essential element but it is only required in relatively small quantities. There are also what are called micronutrients, such as manganese, iron, boron, molybdenum, zinc and copper, which all contribute in some way to the manufacture of chlorophyll and enzymes in the plant. Although these elements are necessary only in minute amounts, deficiencies cause chlorosis (discoloring) of the leaves. A corrective chemical, most often a small quantity of iron or manganese, will quickly rectify the situation and the plant will recover and grow on.

Temperature is another factor that has a vital influence on the growth of plants. In temperate climates plant growth all but ceases below 42°F (6°C). Above this temperature, all other things being equal, growth is more rapid the warmer it is. For most garden plants the optimum temperature for fast growth is around 75 to 85°F (24-29°C), which explains why some plants can make as much growth in one summer's day as in a whole spring month.

At very high temperatures plants cease to grow and conversely at temperatures below freezing point many plants die. Some plants which are often described as tender may survive if they are growing in well-drained soil or if the cold does not last too long. Mulching around the base of a plant may well help it to survive; even if the tops are frosted new shoots will come again from a base that has not been killed.

Light is yet another requirement for healthy plant growth. The sun's energy is converted to chemical energy by the green chlorophyll in leaves, so producing the materials of which plants are made. The leafier the plant is, the quicker it will grow.

Variation in the intensity and duration of light and dark are important factors that influence seed germination and the ability of some plants to flower. There are plants, such as tobacco, which will grow but not flower during a northern European summer because the days are too long. Other plants, including certain crops such as beets and Chinese cabbage, bolt and run to seed before they are ready to pick if they are sown too early in the season.

The intensity of light and shade has a marked effect on the appearance of certain plants. It will affect their height and bulk, and the color intensity of their leaves or flowers. Many blue-colored clematis bleach in the sun, while some variegated plants lose their variegations in the shade.

Sun-loving species will grow wispy in the shade as they reach for the light.

In a garden the range of plants that can be grown is broadly determined by the climate of the area and the character of the soil. The range can be widened by adjusting the soil and, at the right time of the year, by providing protection from heat or cold and by controlling the amount of water that plants receive. Even within one garden, variations in the soil and its moisture content, in the level of light or shade, and in the degree of protection from wind and cold, create several different habitats, in each of which some plants will thrive.

Knowing the country of origin and natural habitat of a plant helps in finding the right place for it in the garden. For example, bulbs such as irises, tulips and nerines are plants respectively of southern Europe, central Asia and southern Africa, in most cases growing in sun-baked conditions. It is pointless growing these plants in shade – for example, overshadowed by tall trees: to thrive they need a dry, sunny position. However, daffodils and bluebells, natives of temperate Europe, flower early, before the leaf canopy of deciduous trees develops, and do well as an underplanting. Most rhododendrons come from forested areas of North America and Asia where summer conditions are reasonably cool and humid and the moist soil is rich in organic matter and very acidic: they are therefore ill suited to dry or chalky soils and areas that have hot dry summers.

Plants from the same or similar habitats will find companionship in each other and look good together. As the requirements of most garden plants are relatively simple, it is not difficult to choose plants that will get along with one another quite happily. However, it is important that these requirements be met if you are to get the best out of your garden in the short and long term.

The two gardens here are both pictured in late spring, but the conditions differ.
Left: On a site where the soil is acidic, flowering trees provide shade for rhododendrons to thrive. These mostly come from mountain regions where the humidity is high and there is never any great heat. The yellow tulips require sun and are furthest from the trees, while the bergenias which surround them are tolerant of a wider range of soils and light conditions.
Above: A contrived alpine bed. Here, bulbs, including *Tulipa* 'Humming Bird' and *Narcissus* 'Hawera' are in full flower; they will ripen well during the summer before starting into growth again toward the end of the year. The small alpine *Phlox subulata* 'Marjorie' also enjoys the good drainage.

These two pages show the development of a border over five years. As with any successful garden, the design is still evolving.

Above: When the garden plot was first acquired, it had a fine stone wall but there were no borders to speak of, and the lawn was rough.

Above right: A year later a border has been created, the old lawn has been partly taken up, the ground leveled and areas of the lawn then resown. This photograph was taken in early summer. The planting still looks thin but there are shrubs to give height and perennials such as irises (not yet in flower) and yellow loosestrife (*Lysimachia punctata*) are starting to get established.

PLANNING FOR GROWTH

The time it takes for a garden to reach maturity depends very much on the speed with which the plants grow. There can be considerable variations from one garden to another, depending on the availability of the essential requirements for growth. However, it is still possible to gain a general impression of the way a garden will mature over, say, a period of twelve years.

If at the planning stage you can visualize how the plants will develop, taking into account their different rates of growth, you should be spared the disappointment of a garden that never attains its full beauty. All too often a plan is devised and plants placed according to it without much thought for the long-term development of the garden. In subsequent years problems are dealt with as they occur – plants are pruned, removed or most frequently left – and the garden never quite achieves its potential. A little thinking ahead will often mean a much shorter and smoother progress to maturity.

It is possible to offer some rough-and-ready generalizations. In the first year, long-term plants – trees, shrubs, perennial border plants and ground cover – will make little growth but annuals will give a good display. By the third year, perennials and ground-cover plants will be well established, some climbers will already require pruning, and fast-growing shrubs will have grown sufficiently to give substance to the garden. The slower-growing bushes and trees will have established their roots and will be ready to push out substantial growth over the next few years.

Far left: In its second year the border looks much fuller. A piece of sculpture has been added to provide a focal point. Gaps in the permanent planting have been filled with short-term plants such as clarkias in shades of pink and apricot, as well as red penstemon and nasturtiums – both these plants are perennials, but they are not fully hardy, so have to be planted out annually.
Near left: In the mature border the planting is almost exclusively of shrubs (complemented by *Cornus controversa* set into the lawn) and perennials such as *Alchemilla mollis*, geraniums, campanula and euphorbia. Some radical changes have been made as the border has developed. A *Robina pseudoacacia* 'Frisia', originally intended as a focal point outside the border, has since been incorporated in it. Also, a *Prunus hillieri* × 'Spire', which did not provide sufficient interest, has been jettisoned from the garden altogether.

Although the mature border illustrated on the previous pages relies heavily on shrubs and perennials in summer, the planting still allows for a spring display of bulbs. Tulips, in various colors, are the star performers here. They can be planted in late autumn, after the perennials have died back. If left in the border, they would be unlikely to give a second season of flower. A better course would be to lift them before growth becomes too dense and allow them to ripen and die down in some other, spare corner of the garden. Infill planting like this needs as much care as long-term planting. For example, judicious selection of tulips can ensure a relatively long display, with species tulips occupying center-stage early on and tall-growing cultivars taking over later.

After six years the garden will be showing real signs of becoming established. Hedges will have filled out, and after they have been clipped you will be able to see something approaching their ultimate shape. Climbers will provide a substantial vertical element, and annual pruning will be needed to keep them within bounds. Shrubs will also require pruning to encourage flowering, to keep plants shapely and to check growth that might overwhelm less vigorous neighbors. By this stage herbaceous perennials and other ground cover will need to have been split up and replanted.

At nine years nearly all plants other than trees will have reached their desired size, giving the garden a look of poised maturity. The garden may not change dramatically over the next three years, but by the time that it is in its prime some shrubs may already have been taken out and replaced, and further replanting will be in hand.

Now, having spent an hour or so applying these basic guidelines to the garden you have provisionally in mind, and visualizing how the garden will develop over a period of twelve years, you should think back on your choice of plants. It may be sensible to substitute for some of the most vigorous among your initial selection, which might swamp slow-growing plants, others of more moderate growth so that each year the garden has a balanced and unified appearance. On the other hand, if you want quicker results, fast-growing plants could be substituted for those that make slow growth or, alternatively, larger and more mature plants could be used rather than young nursery stock. However, large plants cost more, and a further disadvantage is that there is a lower success rate than when planting young specimens. More details and other strategies for instant effect and interim measures are described in the section on Timely Solutions (pp. 77-89).

For a fairly large garden a time-scale of twelve years from planting to maturity is reasonable, but in a smaller garden or courtyard a mature effect can be achieved in three or four years. The confined space makes it unnecessary to depend so much on trees and large shrubs, and more reliance can be placed on smaller plants and those grown in pots.

Whatever the size of the garden, if you are growing trees and hedges it is as well to give them as early a start as possible. They are generally the slowest-growing of the plants you will want, yet they are usually key features of the design. It is not only a matter of the time it takes for the plants to reach a certain size, it is also a question of flowering. Although some flowering trees and shrubs, for example *Magnolia stellata*, will bloom at a very early stage of their development, many others that are highly desirable – including *M. grandiflora*, *Davidia involucrata* and *Chimonanthus praecox* – take from six to ten years to flower. These are not trees for those in a hurry, but they are well worth waiting for, and add much to the character of a garden.

To economize on time or money you may choose to phase the planting over several years, but starting with those plants that are most important to the design, slowest-growing or slowest to come into flower so that the garden reaches full maturity as soon as possible. It will not necessarily be possible to plant everything in absolutely the right order, partly because nurseries or garden centers may not have stock available when you want it; however, you should keep as close as you can to an ordered program. Remember that with some plants you need both male and female specimens if you are to get a display of fruit. This is true, for example, of hollies (*Ilex*) and skimmias. Many fruit trees, including apples, pears and sweet cherries, will fail to produce good crops if a variety is planted where there is no pollinating variety nearby. Your planning has to take factors such as these into account if you are to get the results you want.

Plants that reach maturity relatively quickly pose a practical problem, as they need to be kept in shape while the rest of the garden matures. This is where a knowledge of pruning and general maintenance of plants is all-important. A key principle to understand is that the more severely you prune vigorous shoots, the more strongly each remaining bud is subsequently going to grow. Removing the largest branch that is upsetting the balance of a shrub will, in the long term, produce a result exactly the opposite of what you might expect, encouraging the growth of more branches and so accentuating the imbalance.

The secret of success is to begin by buying healthy-looking specimens with good symmetrical growth. Once plants are in the garden you must keep an eye on their development; as soon as you notice any unevenness in the branches, cut the weakest ones hard back and the most vigorous ones lightly.

Pruning can also be used to maintain the juvenile stage of a plant that if left to mature would take on a different habit as an adult plant. Ivy (*Hedera*), *Euonymus*, holm oak (*Quercus ilex*) and junipers (*Juniperus*) are among the most commonly grown plants that have markedly different juvenile and adult foliage, a phenomenon known as dimorphism. However, the main purpose of pruning is to control excessive growth and to promote flowering and fruiting. It is probably the most important strategy available to the gardener for manipulating the growth of plants; see pp. 19, 26, 33 for more information.

GROWTH RATES

The growth charts on the following pages show stages in the development of a selection of plants within four main categories: trees, shrubs, climbers and ground cover.

The trees, shrubs and climbers are depicted at planting time and then at three, six and twelve years old, showing also the seasonal changes.

Planting of deciduous trees and shrubs is depicted in winter: this is the correct time for planting deciduous woody plants, as growth is dormant. Evergreens should be planted in early to mid-spring, as growth starts much later.

The three-year-old specimens show the spring characteristics of deciduous trees and shrubs; the six-year-old ones show the summer characteristics; and the twelve-year-old ones show the autumn characteristics.

Ground-cover plants, which include evergreens and herbaceous perennials, are illustrated at planting time and then at two years, when they should be just touching, and finally at four years, when they are covering the ground adequately to suppress weed growth.

The heights and spreads given are "horticultural": this means that they take into account pruning where and when necessary. They are only an approximate average, as growth can vary tremendously.

The conditions in which a plant is grown are all-important. For example, in a hot and sunny climate where either the humidity or rainfall is high or where plentiful irrigation is available, growth can be nearly twice as much in a season as in a colder, duller climate, or where water is scarce. At the other end of the year, a mild winter, when growth scarcely stops, means that a plant will achieve much greater heights than if it had been severely knocked back by prolonged freezing temperatures.

A planting of evergreen and deciduous trees and shrubs that have matured over twenty years creates a composition of all-year interest. The garden includes *Fagus sylvatica* 'Dawyck' (rear, right, in this picture), yew topiary, *Pieris forestii* (with young pink growth). In the middle ground are white-flowering *Hebe cupressoides* and two slow-growing conifers, *Chamaecyparis obtusa* 'Nana Gracilis' (right) and *Picea glauca* 'Albertiana Conica' (left). In the foreground are *Spiraea* × *bumalda* 'Gold Flame' and (at the left of the picture) *Chamaecyparis lawsoniana* 'Lane' – one of the best golden Lawsons.

Trees live as long as, or longer than we do, and in their full maturity they give to a garden an air of timelessness that no other plants can create. They are the most important plants for forming the green vertical dimension of a garden, and by their stature and mass they give solidity to a design. Individual trees may have several qualities that make them worth growing – pleasing form, attractive foliage, showy flowers and fruit, handsome bark or colored twigs – and in the garden many provide much-needed shade.

Although trees have so much to recommend them, many gardeners are put off planting them, partly because of the time many take to make significant growth, partly because it is not easy to find room for a tree in a small garden. However, the range of trees worth growing is so vast, including some that are fast-growing and many which at maturity are small or medium in size, that impatient gardeners and those with small gardens have plenty from which to choose. Those illustrated have been chosen for their relatively small stature (although no dwarfs have been included). Some, for example *Sorbus aucuparia*, *Robinia pseudoacacia* 'Frisia' and *Malus tschonoskii*, are reasonably fast-growing, reaching more than 22 feet (7m) in twelve years. Thereafter their growth slows down and their ultimate height is no more than 30 to 40 feet (9-12m). But the Leyland cypress will grow very fast to 30 feet (9m) in the first twelve years of its life and is most useful for providing quick screens, as are birch, alder, poplars and sycamore.

At the other extreme there are slow-growing trees such as *Magnolia stellata* and the Japanese maples (*Acer japonicum* and *A. palmatum*), which never reach great heights and are sometimes grouped with shrubs. The largest trees which form the high canopy of a woodland – including beech, ash, sweet chestnut, horse chestnut, firs, pines and oak – are slow-growing and may take many years to reach their ultimate height but are only suitable for larger gardens.

In choosing a tree for a small garden pay particular attention to shape. A columnar specimen – one that has vertical branches close together – will be most useful for a narrow space; look out for cultivars bearing the names 'Fastigiata' or 'Columnaris'.

TREES

The maples are among the best trees for small gardens with acid to neutral soils. *Acer palmatum* 'Atro-purpureum' grows to about 6 feet (1.8m) in ten years, if it is grown in a sheltered position in well-drained, moisture-retentive soil. Here, a young specimen displays its fiery autumn colors.

There is no unanimous opinion on the distance to allow between a building and a newly planted tree. Tree roots undoubtedly can cause serious damage to the foundations of buildings and to drains, although it is also true that trees are sometimes blamed when other factors should be taken into account. It has been suggested that no tree should be closer to a house than its height at maturity, but we have a linden 90 feet (27m) high and over a hundred years old, only 20 feet (6m) from the house, without any signs of damage: the greatest problem is the light it cuts out from the kitchen and the sticky droppings from the aphids that inhabit it all summer. The dangers posed by

trees near buildings depend to some extent on species or variety and on the nature of the soil and the site. Willows, for example, have particularly questing roots that can do considerable damage to drains. Shallow-rooted trees, such as many of the pines, stand a much greater risk of being blown over if they are planted on light soil in exposed positions. A knowledge of your tree and your site has to be combined with common sense. To some extent, pruning can be used to contain a tree, but if it becomes clear that you have made a mistake, cut the tree down before it becomes unmanageable.

In general, though, you should think long and hard before taking the drastic step of felling mature trees. (Bear in mind too that there may be legal restrictions on their removal.) If you are tempted to have trees removed because of the shade they cast, consider creating a woodland garden, in which you can grow plants that thrive in shady conditions, or a spring garden, in which many of the plants will flower before the leaves of deciduous trees are fully out. Where the shade cast by a tree is a problem, it is often possible to thin the canopy considerably. This will not greatly affect the tree's general appearance but will let in more light and reduce the number of leaves shed in autumn, the clearing of which is an annual chore. A major thinning job should be carried out by a specialist tree surgeon, who will have all the necessary tools and safety equipment. The pruning that should begin at an early stage in a tree's development is, however, a form of thinning. Cut out crossing branches and any dead or diseased ones to maintain a good shape, and "rub out" any shoots on the trunk to prevent low branches from developing.

If a large tree in the garden dies, it may seem like a good idea to use the skeleton to support a climber such as a rambler rose. But a dead stump can harbor certain types of fungus. Furthermore, the space taken up by a stump can generally be put to better use. If the removal looks a daunting task, call in a qualified arboriculturist.

The expense of having the entire stump and roots of the tree removed is worthwhile because anything that remains may all too easily become a seat of infection.

ROBINIA PSEUDOACACIA 'FRISIA'

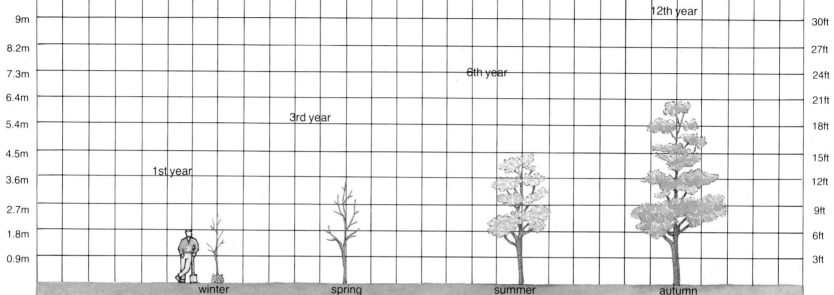

SORBUS ARIA

PRUNUS × SUBHIRTELLA 'AUTUMNALIS'

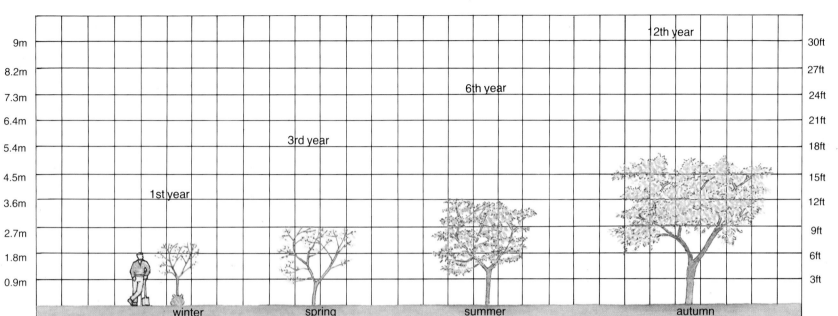

9m — 30ft
8.2m — 27ft
7.3m — 24ft
6.4m — 21ft
5.4m — 18ft
4.5m — 15ft
3.6m — 12ft
2.7m — 9ft
1.8m — 6ft
0.9m — 3ft

12th year

6th year

3rd year

1st year

winter   spring   summer   autumn

SORBUS AUCUPARIA

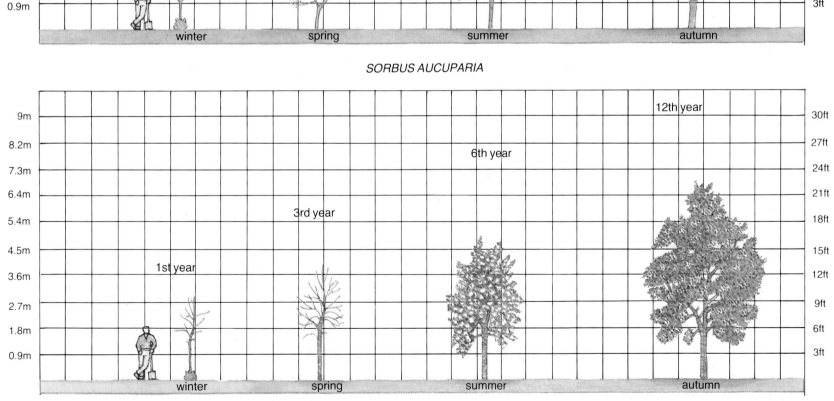

9m — 30ft
8.2m — 27ft
7.3m — 24ft
6.4m — 21ft
5.4m — 18ft
4.5m — 15ft
3.6m — 12ft
2.7m — 9ft
1.8m — 6ft
0.9m — 3ft

12th year

6th year

3rd year

1st year

winter   spring   summer   autumn

LABURNUM × *WATERERI* 'VOSSII'

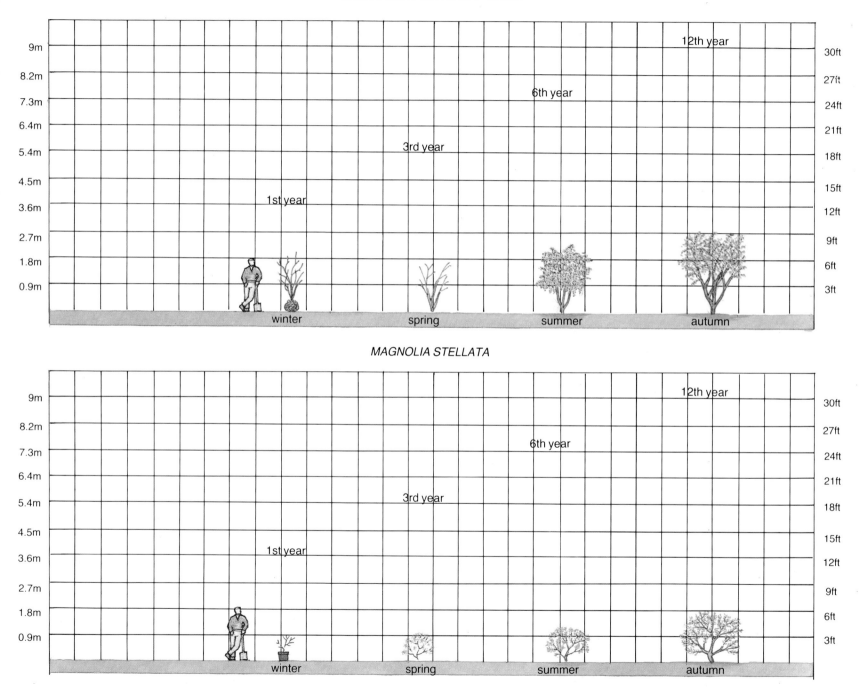

MAGNOLIA STELLATA

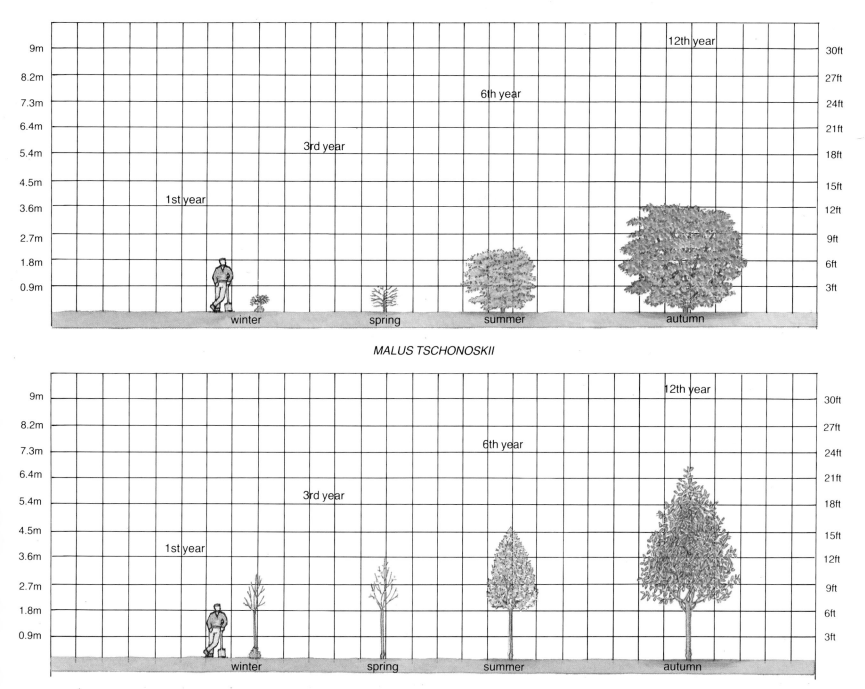

ACER PALMATUM

MALUS TSCHONOSKII

METASEQUOIA GLYPTOSTROBOIDES

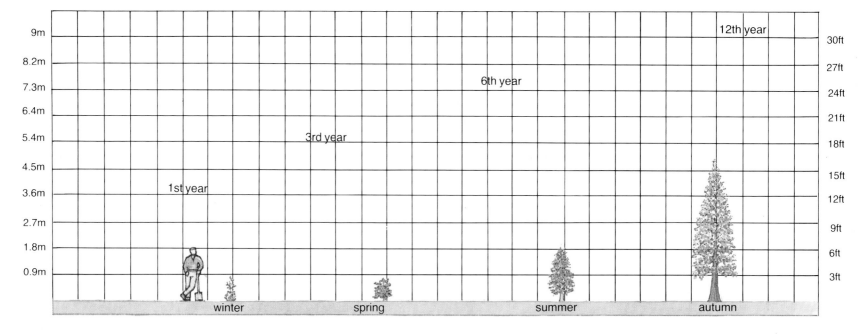

x CUPRESSOCYPARIS LEYLANDII

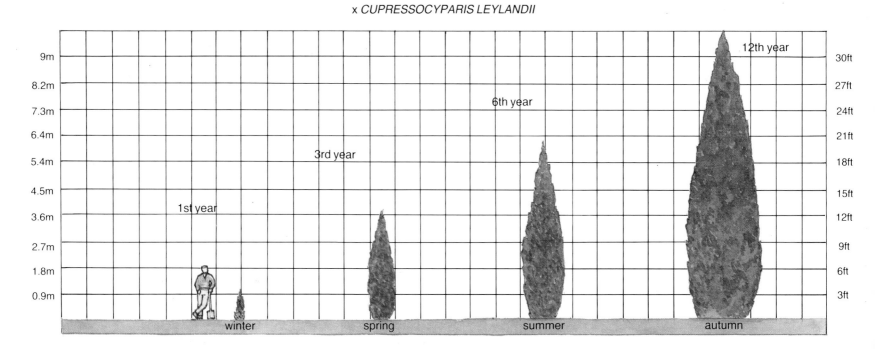

Prunus × *subhirtella* 'Autumnalis' performs well all year.

Climbers and wall shrubs are curiously under-valued and yet they can extend even the smallest garden into the vertical dimension. The structure for that dimension can be provided by purpose-built pergolas, arbors or trellis obelisks, to be clothed with handsome foliage plants or billowing masses of flowers such as roses and clematis. More often than not, the vertical dimension is already there in the form of walls and fences. A choice climber or wall shrub, slightly tender perhaps, as many are, is just the thing to highlight a beautiful old sunny wall; while ugly walls and buildings, including those in shade, can be transformed into major features of a garden when they are well furnished with good plants. Climbers can work themselves through shrubs or even be sent up into tall trees so that the supports are involved in what becomes a double performance.

When choosing a climber for a particular position, you need to consider whether it is self-clinging (like ivy and Virginia creeper) or needs support for twining stems or tendrils. Some people think that self-clinging climbers damage the mortar in brick and stone walls. But provided that the mortar is sound to begin with, these climbers will not appreciably accelerate its natural deterioration, and the protection they give to a wall more than compensates for any damage they may do.

Climbers that twine or use tendrils to hoist themselves up must be given an adequate means of support. If the support is to be another plant, this must be matched to the vigor of the climber trained into it. Where the support is to be trellis or wires, these need to be well secured and extend far enough to take the climber at its mature size. When a climber runs out of support it tends to double back, making a tangled mass. The weight of the vegetation may then pull down the supports, so that the whole plant flops over, creating an unsightly muddle. Although many wall shrubs need little or no support, those of rather languid growth need to be tied in.

Climbers in particular vary considerably in their vigor and they need to be well chosen for their purpose and the space available to them. Among the most vigorous are the Russian vine, the crimson glory vine and even such roses as *Rosa filipes* 'Kiftsgate' and 'Albéric Barbier'.

CLIMBERS AND WALL SHRUBS

Clematis are among the most useful flowering climbers. The species and varieties cover a long flowering season and, while many are vigorous, there are also some that are slow-growing. The large-flowered cultivar 'Perle d'Azur', which flowers all summer if pruned hard in early spring, will climb to a height of about 12 feet (3.6m). It thrives in alkaline soil.

Some of these strong growers will push on to 90 feet (27m), having reached a third of that height in ten to twelve years. In contrast are more gentle climbers that will barely achieve 8 feet (2.4m) in twelve years and scarcely more thereafter. These include some of the so-called pillar roses, such as 'Royal Gold' and 'Aloha', and less familar climbers such as *Actinidia kolomikta* and *Trachelospermum asiaticum*. Allowance must be made for lateral growth. There are climbers and wall shrubs that naturally tend to spread outward, and some are more easily trained to do so than others.

Because walls, fences and even other plants used as supports create their own rain shadow, the ground in which climbers and wall shrubs are to be planted needs to be well prepared in advance with the addition of moisture-retentive organic matter. Allow a good foot (30cm) between the planting hole and the wall or fence behind it, and when planting spread the roots out toward the garden. The less vigorous climbers and wall shrubs in particular will need watering and regular feeding in their early stages if they are to thrive. Tie plants in as they develop, firmly securing them to their supports.

As with shrubs, the main operation in maintaining climbers and wall shrubs is pruning. The aims are not only to maintain their health and flowering potential but also to train them and to curb the most vigorous. Many of these will make considerable growth even in the first season; and in subsequent years, if there is no training or pruning, there is a risk of them causing damage. Tiles can be dislodged, drains and gutters blocked, window hinges distorted and paint work spoiled. Wisteria, rambling roses and ivies as well as *Vitis* and *Parthenocissus* species are all climbers that can cause problems if they are not adequately trained and pruned.

In the initial stages pruning should encourage the plant to cover a specific area. In the dormant season make judicious cuts above buds pointing in the direction where growth is wanted. This pruning will cause the buds to break and the growth can eventually be trained to fill the vacant area. As wall shrubs and the more restrained climbers become established, remove any dying or diseased wood and any branches that cross or are growing away from the wall. This annual pruning I find easiest to do when I am deadheading spent flowers. At the end of winter, if the plant is getting bare at the base, I cut out one or two of the oldest stems right down to the base in order to stimulate strong new growth.

Stronger-growing climbers will almost certainly need cutting back to contain them in their allotted space. The most drastic pruning should be done during the winter, but I often find myself fine-tuning throughout the growing season. Every time I pass a plant in my garden and see a branch that is overstepping its mark, I like to cut it there and then.

PYRANCANTHA COCCINEA

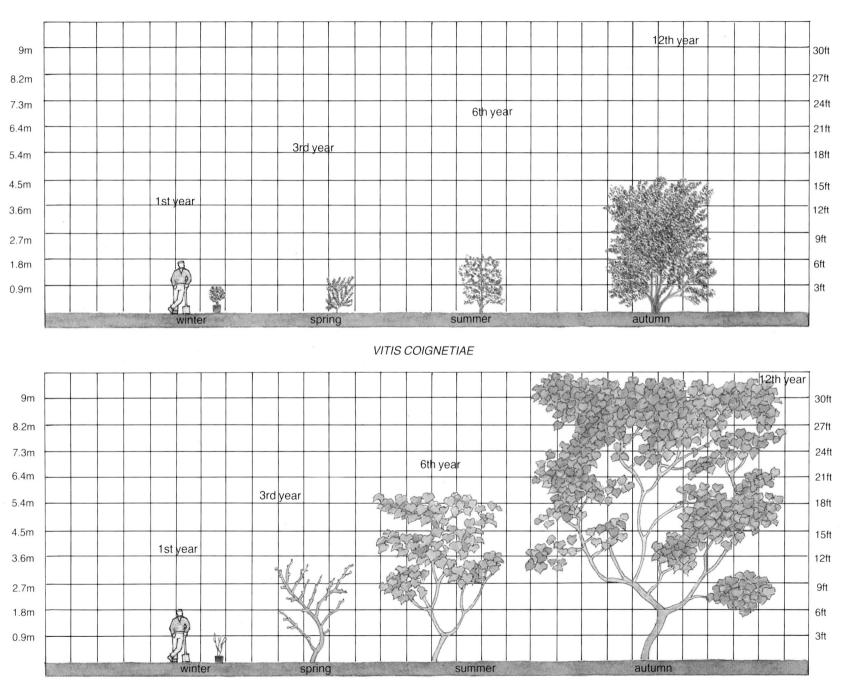

VITIS COIGNETIAE

HEDERA COLCHICA 'DENTATA VARIEGATA'

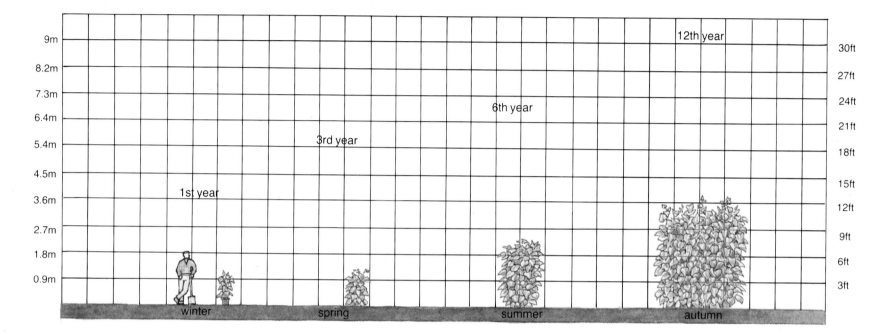

PARTHENOCISSUS QUINQUEFOLIA

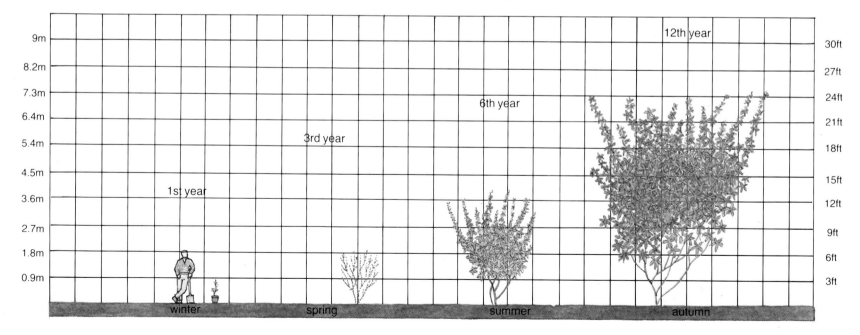

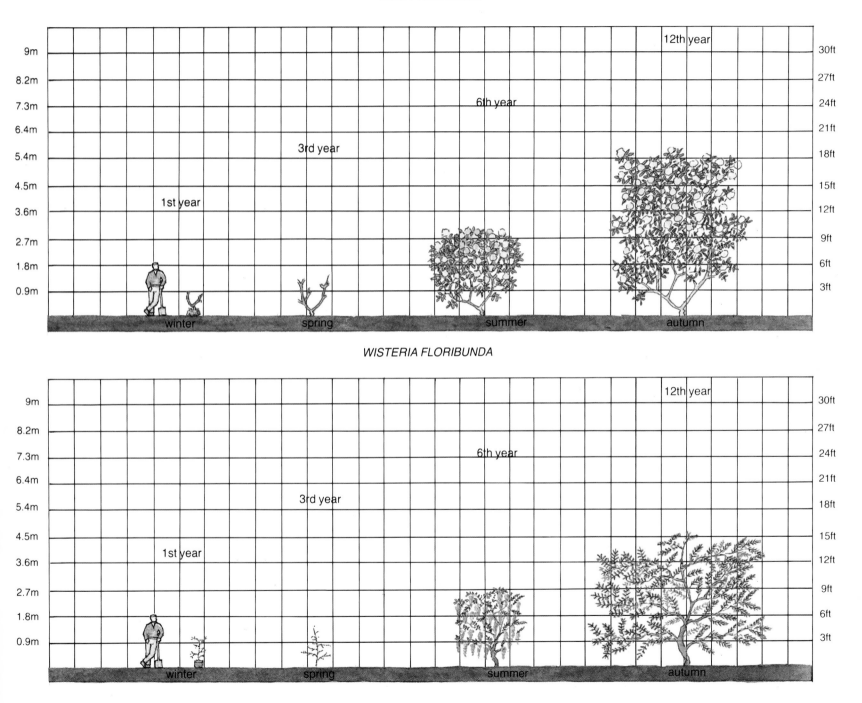

ROSA 'NEW DAWN'

WISTERIA FLORIBUNDA

CLEMATIS MONTANA

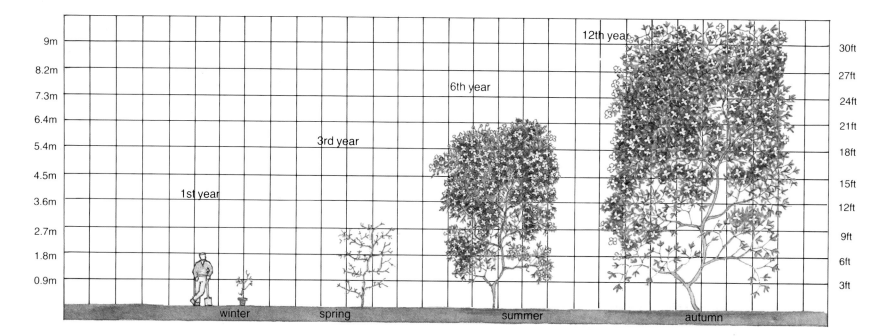

CHIMONANTHUS PRAECOX

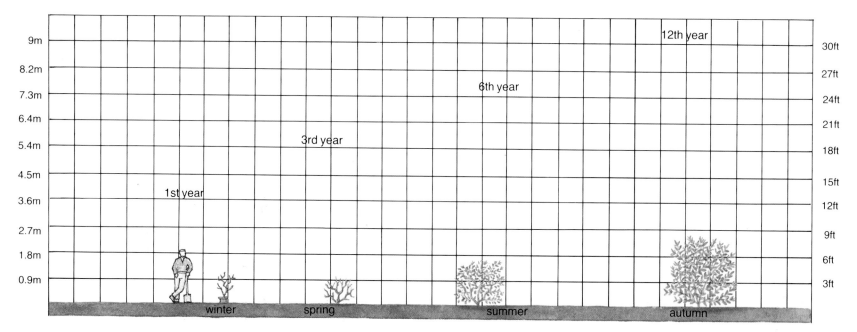

HYDRANGEA PETIOLARIS

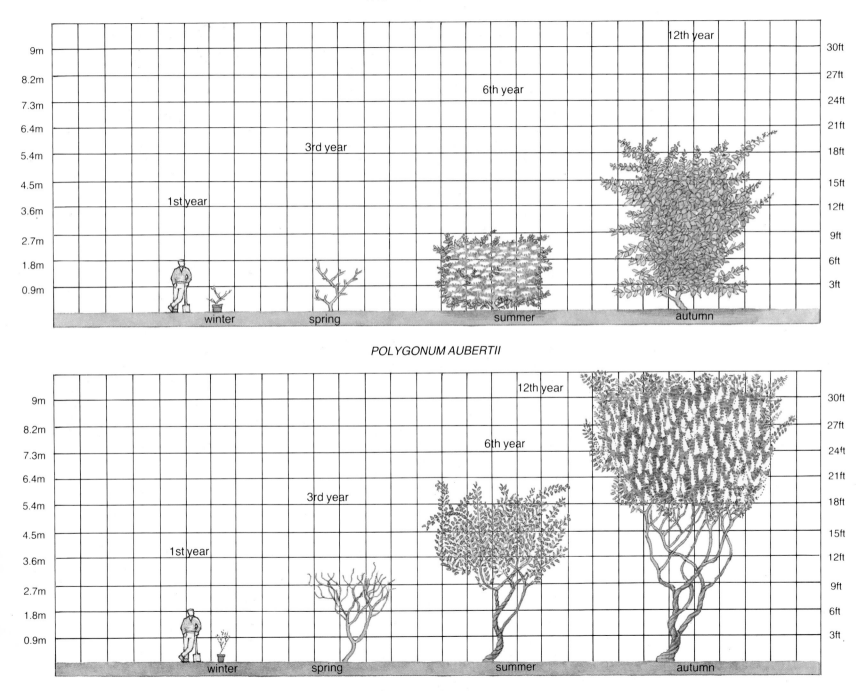

POLYGONUM AUBERTII

There are vigorous climbers that can completely transform buildings and structures, engulfing them in dense foliage. Boston ivy (*Parthenocissus tricuspidata*), which here shrouds an old summer house, turns a deep shade of crimson in the autumn. This species needs to be kept in check to prevent it from covering windows and damaging roofs and gutters.

There are very good reasons for shrubs to form the backbone planting of many gardens. They are generally reasonably long-lived, a large number are of sufficient size to give body to a garden, on the whole they are not difficult plants, and many are outstanding ornamentals. They can be grouped with other shrubs to create shrubberies, used with herbaceous perennials and bulbs in mixed borders, or the finest among them can be planted in isolation to show off their special qualities.

There are shrubs for all soil types. Camellia, pieris, kalmia and rhododendrons require moisture-retentive, acidic soils; brooms, rock roses, daphnes and lavender thrive best in highly alkaline soils.

At one end of the size range are substantial plant such as *Pyracantha* 'Mojave' and lilac (*Syringa vulgaris*), both of which can reach 10 feet (3m) in the first twelve years of growth; at the other end are diminutive examples such as *Arctostaphylos uva-ursi* and *Cotoneaster adpressus*, which never grow more than 6 inches (15 cm) high. Most lie somewhere between, many reaching 8 feet (2.4m) or so at maturity. The size range means that there is a shrub for almost every situation in the garden. In a shrub border, for example, medium-sized to large plants may make up the core with smaller, slower-growing ones positioned at the front.

The charts depict two evergreen shrubs and eight deciduous, four spring- and four summer-flowering. These provide a very small sample of the exceptional range of attributes to be found among shrubs. You can see how some have autumn color in fruit and foliage, and you will find in the Directory (p. 157) some variegated forms and some grown for their winter bark effect as well as others that are more conventionally appealing.

To maintain shrubs in good shape and to get the maximum display from them year after year you will need to prune them regularly. Usually, aiming for the first of these requirements will satisfy the second, and, when the plant has established itself (after four or five years in the garden), pruning need only be done once a year. As a general rule, shrubs that flower in the spring do so on the previous year's wood. Pruning should be done immediately after

SHRUBS

As foliage and flowering plants of substance, shrubs are invaluable in providing an enduring backbone to the garden. Careful grouping can enhance individual qualities, creating attractive combinations of color, shape and texture. Here, at the height of summer, the colorful and richly textured combination includes the grey leaves of *Senecio* 'Sunshine', the smaller yellow leaves of *Lonicera pileata*, the pink flowers of *Spiraea* × *bumalda* and the white ones of *Hydrangea paniculata*.

flowering to give the plant maximum time to grow sufficient wood for the following year's flowers. But remember that if you cut all the flower stems off, you will have no fruit in the autumn. If the fruits themselves are decorative, prune out only half or a third of the flowering stems. Summer-flowering shrubs generally bloom on the current year's wood. If a fairly radical cut is required, prune at the end of summer or at the beginning of spring. Shrubs grown for the effect of their bark in the winter should be pruned hard back in the spring.

Throughout the life of the shrub you should look out for weak and diseased or dead branches, and cut these out and burn them immediately to prevent the spread of disease. Keep the shape of the shrub balanced by cutting any awkwardly placed branch right down to the main stem. Be bold in your pruning; if you trim timidly you will end up with a topiary specimen that bears no resemblance to the shrub you planted.

Although a shrubbery will take recognizable shape quite early, it will reach its prime only after about ten to twelve years. Then each plant should still retain its characteristic shape but will be just about to touch the shrubs next to it. The shrubbery will continue to look its best for another five years, after which it will begin to show its age. Its life will depend on two main factors: the rate of growth of individual plants and the density of planting. Although ideally distance between shrubs at planting time should be based on the probable spread twelve years on, it is generally worth planting slightly more closely in order to obtain a solid effect more quickly. This will require pruning of the most vigorous specimens to keep them within bounds. In the early stages, before much growth has been made, and in order to keep the weeds down, the spaces between shrubs must be furnished with bulbs, ground-covering plants and some annuals, always remembering to remove the fillers when they are no longer needed.

If there is still some space between the shrubs where weeds may sow themselves, carefully apply small quantities of a pre-emergence herbicide (see glossary): most (but not all) shrubs) will be unaffected by this.

RHODODENDRON LUTEUM

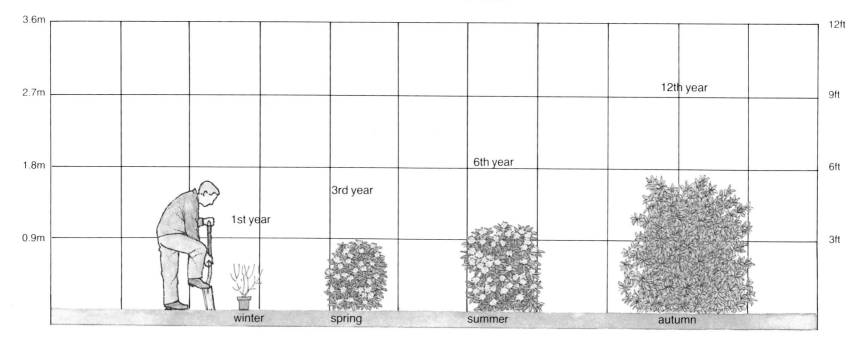

HAMAMELIS MOLLIS

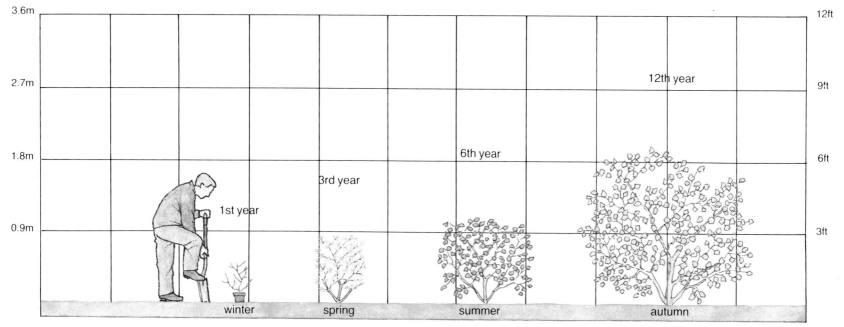

RHODODENDRON YAKUSHIMANUM

3.6m — 12ft
2.7m — 9ft

12th year

6th year

1.8m — 6ft

3rd year

1st year

0.9m — 3ft

winter   spring   summer   autumn

VIBURNUM TINUS

3.6m — 12ft
2.7m — 9ft

12th year

1.8m — 6ft

6th year

3rd year

1st year

0.9m — 3ft

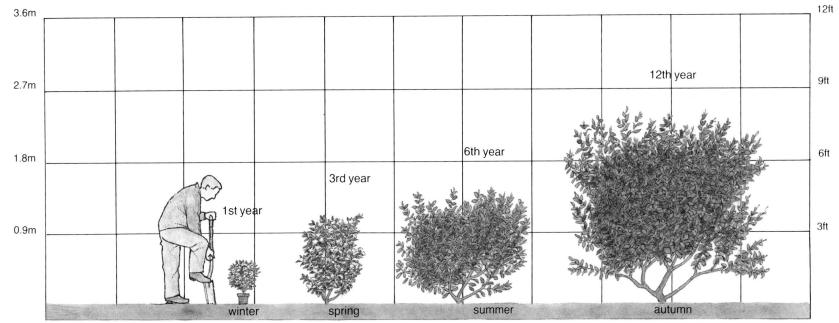

winter   spring   summer   autumn

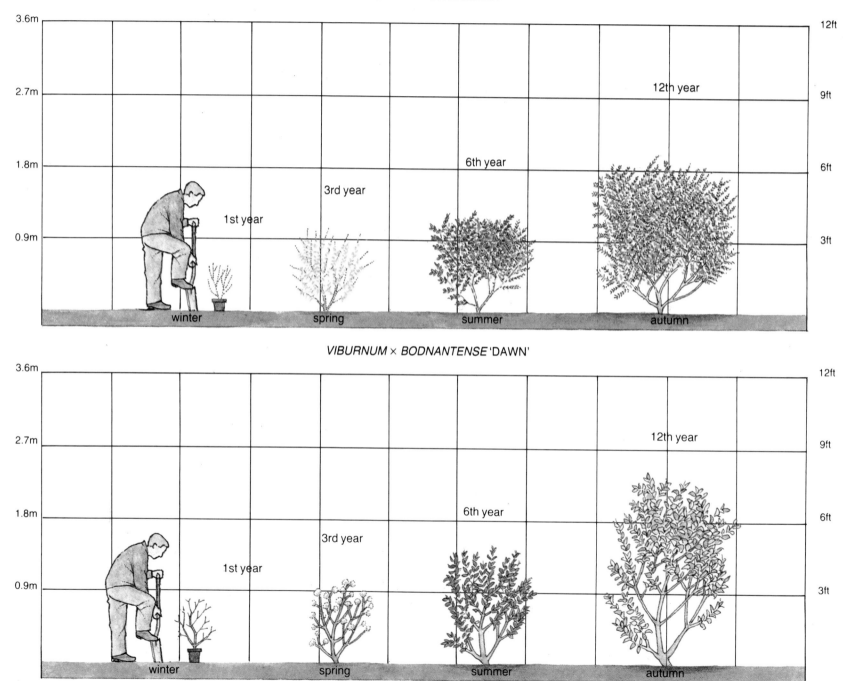

FORSYTHIA × INTERMEDIA

VIBURNUM × BODNANTENSE 'DAWN'

BUDDLEJA ALTERNIFOLIA

PHILADELPHUS 'VIRGINAL'

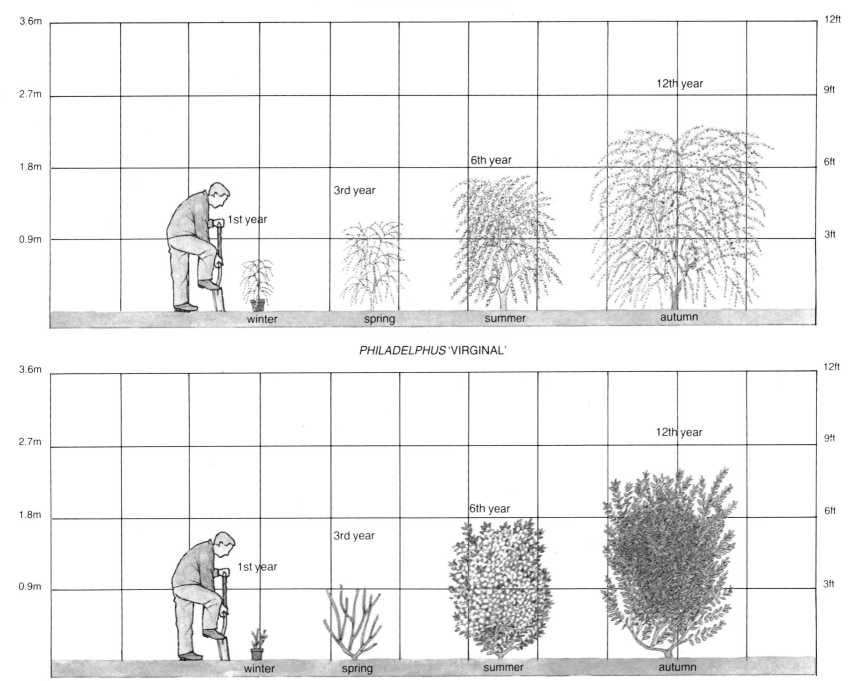

ROSA GLAUCA

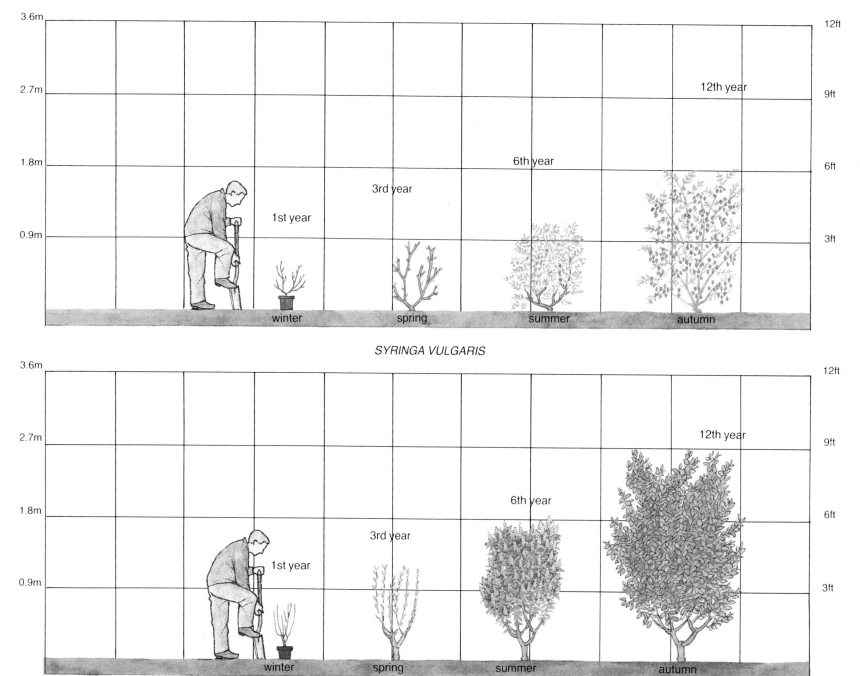

SYRINGA VULGARIS

Ground-cover plants are low-growing, speedy spreaders, forming dense carpets that smother weeds and therefore reduce the workload in the garden. Their attraction, however, goes far beyond being simply practical. Many ground-cover plants are highly ornamental, and when they are skillfully planted they can make a varied and interesting picture in the garden throughout the year. By definition they must produce a large quantity of leaves, and these come in all shapes, sizes and textures. There are large heart-shaped leaves and tiny round leaves, some are smooth and shiny, while others have a dull, hairy texture. Colors range from dark green to palest yellow green through metallic blue, and there are innumerable variegated permutations.

These plants are a positive alternative, or complement, to grass, the ultimate ground cover, over which they have certain advantages. Provided the right choice is made, they can be planted where mowing would be difficult and where, because of shade or poor soil, grass would not grow. The initial cost of purchasing the plants is relatively low, and they are not difficult to plant. They increase at differing speeds, depending on the type of plants and the conditions in which they are placed.

In comparison with grass, however, ground-cover plants have some disadvantages. At the outset they are more expensive to buy, and more time and labor is needed to plant the same area. During the establishment period it is necessary to weed them – this requires care, particularly with creeping ground cover, where it is all too easy to cut back the very plants that you are hoping will spread. And, subsequently, tree seedlings, which germinate readily in the undisturbed moist soil under the ground cover, may become a problem, and must be removed by hand.

A word of caution is called for. Creeping ground cover, which propagates itself either by stolons or by underground shoots, may become a menace, spreading relentlessly and swamping any other small structural or ground-cover plants you may try to include in the scheme. You will see from the charts, for example, that one plant of *Lamium maculatum* will cover a square 3 feet by 3 feet (90 x 90cm) in four years, provided it has moist ground; but that six plants

GROUND-COVER PLANTS

Good ground-cover plants are reasonably quick to form dense, weed-proof carpets. In this garden a deeply lobed form of the common ivy (*Hedera helix*) makes ideal cover in the shade of a large tree, where it would be difficult to establish grass.

of the form 'Aureum' would be required to cover the same area in the same time. Clump formers vary equally from species to species. Six to seven plants of *Festuca glauca* are necessary to fill the 3 feet (90cm) square but only two of *Hosta albomarginata*.

Getting the planting density right is of crucial importance. The aim should be to obtain cover fast enough to suppress weeds while ensuring that the plants retain their characteristic profile. You should plan to have each plant barely touchings its neighbors after two to three years and fully covering the area after four to five. In subsequent years a mat of vegetation will build up beneath the foliage, slowly decomposing as new growth is generated and forming a dense barrier to any herbaceous weeds.

I find Graham Stuart Thomas's authoritative book *Plants for Ground-cover* invaluable for guidance on planting distances. I also know from observation of ground-cover trial plots that dense planting to achieve a quick result is not successful. The competition between plants is too great and some die off, leaving unsightly patches of dead vegetation. It makes no more sense planting very sparingly. There will be too much competition from weeds, and having to deal with this will defeat the purpose of growing ground cover.

Furthermore, as the ground-cover plants spread, they will, rather like soft cookies on a baking tray, lose their identity and character, which are chief among the qualities for which these plants are grown.

Some of the most exciting combinations of ground-cover plants I have seen include a long edging of lady's mantle (*Alchemilla mollis*) with catmint (*Nepeta* × *faassenii*); hostas in abundance, from the blue-leaved *H. sieboldiana* 'Elegans' to the golden-leaved cultivar 'Sun Power' and *H. albomarginata*, with narrow variegated leaves; Solomon's seal (*Polygonatum* × *hybridum*) with shuttlecock ferns (*Matteuccia struthiopteris*) and American skunk cabbage (*Lysichiton americanum*); and *Sedum* 'Autumn Joy', between the graceful grass *Pennisetum alopecuroides* and the silver *Artemisia* 'Powis Castle'. All these combinations make bold and positive displays which last from early spring through to autumn.

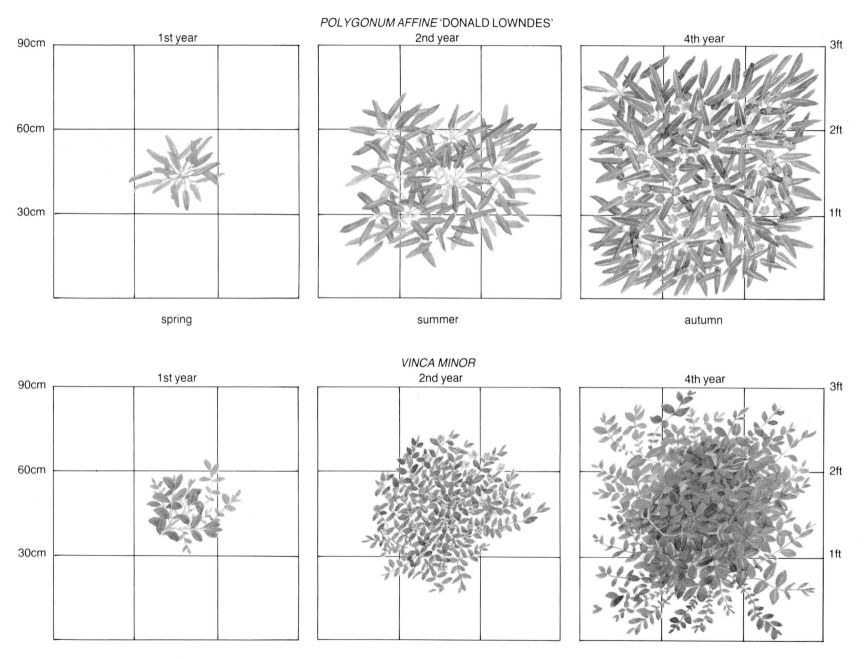

POLYGONUM AFFINE 'DONALD LOWNDES'

1st year	2nd year	4th year

90cm 60cm 30cm

3ft 2ft 1ft

spring summer autumn

VINCA MINOR

1st year	2nd year	4th year

90cm 60cm 30cm

3ft 2ft 1ft

spring summer autumn

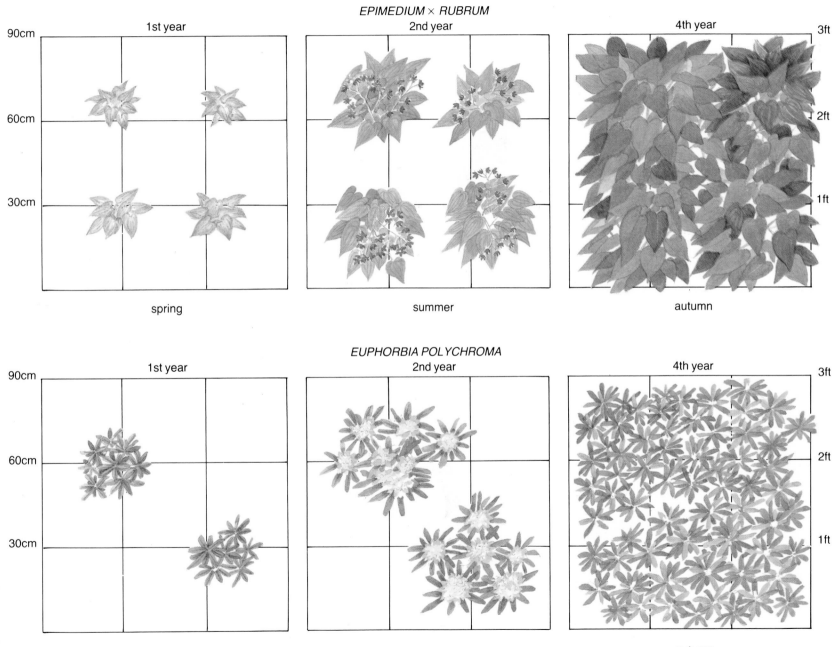

EPIMEDIUM × RUBRUM

1st year	2nd year	4th year
spring	summer	autumn

EUPHORBIA POLYCHROMA

1st year	2nd year	4th year
spring	summer	autumn

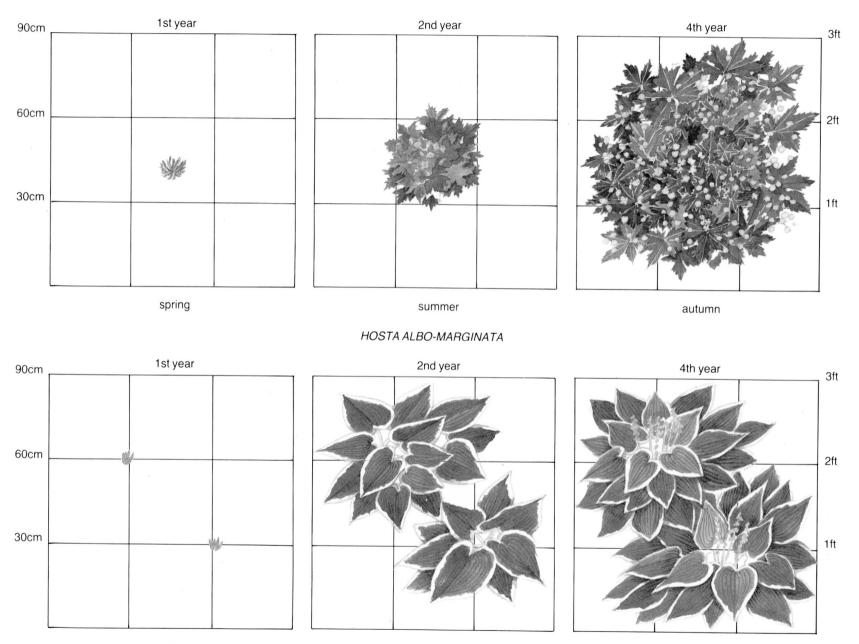

GERANIUM ENDRESSII

1st year — spring
2nd year — summer
4th year — autumn

HOSTA ALBO-MARGINATA

1st year — spring
2nd year — summer
4th year — autumn

FESTUCA GLAUCA

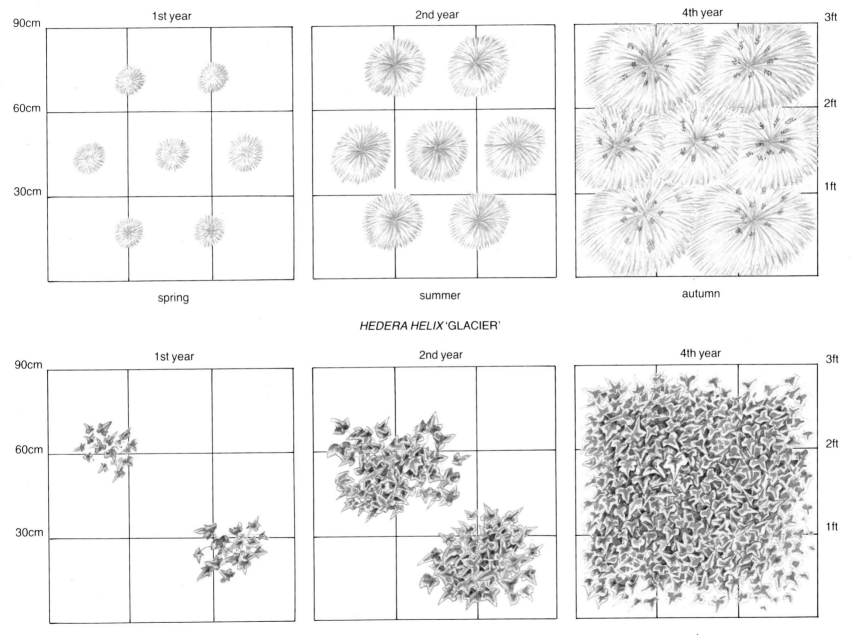

HEDERA HELIX 'GLACIER'

JUNIPERUS HORIZONTALIS 'GREY PEARL'

1st year	2nd year	4th year

spring   summer   autumn

PACHYSANDRA TERMINALIS

1st year	2nd year	4th year

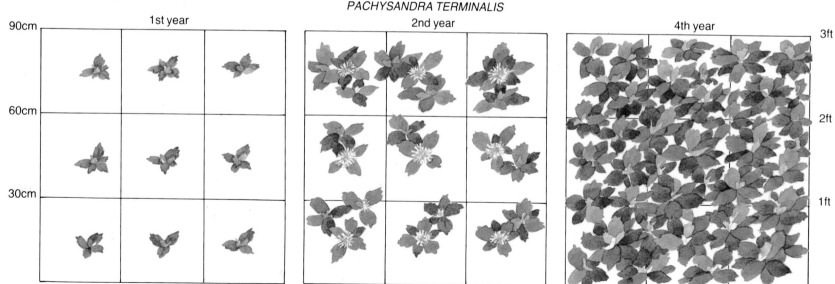

spring   summer   autumn

There are ground-cover plants for almost all conditions. Here, hostas contrast with iris leaves, yellow trollius and red euphorbias.

HEDGES

Hedges, walls, fences, and trellis panels clothed with climbers can all be used to create physical and visual barriers around or within a garden. The function of these may simply be to form boundaries and to establish secluded areas. However, when handled imaginatively, the private enclosure can have all the romantic charm of a secret garden.

My first choice for the boundaries of a secret garden or even of a more practical enclosure would always be solid formal hedges. If I could not have these, my next preference would be for informal screens of shrubs and small trees.

Among the many plants, both deciduous and evergreen, that are suitable for hedging there is considerable variation in growth rates. Some that are fast-growing will form screens 8 feet (2.4m) high, a good height for any hedge, in less than 6 to 8 years. Inevitably, however, the fast growers require several cuts during the year to keep them in trim and at the required height. Hedge trimming can be a major job, so it may be better to choose hedging plants that require only a single cut per year, even though they may take two to four years longer than other plants to reach an adequate height.

Privet (*Ligustrum ovalifolium*) and *Nothofagus antarctica* give quick results and for those in a great hurry there is the ubiquitous Leyland cypress (x *Cupressocyparis leylandii*). This needs more clipping than the other two species and unless pruned early in its life it will become leggy and will not form a dense screen. Traditional long-lived hedging plants include beech (*Fagus sylvatica*), box (*Buxus sempervirens*) and yew (*Taxus baccata*), and hedges of these materials planted several

A semi-circular hedge of copper beech provides shelter and a backdrop for a garden seat. In early summer (left) the metallic-blue foliage of a pot-grown Atlantic cedar stands out well against the deep red foliage of the hedge. The pale green box ball contrasts well with the gaunt shape of the cedar. In late summer (below) the tones are much more muted. The box has been trimmed; the beech, which has not yet had its annual cut, still has a fuzzy outline.

centuries ago are often seen in old gardens. Sometimes they are derelict, overgrown and out of shape, but it is possible to rejuvenate these old hedges by pruning them hard back in the spring.

The culture of a hedge is not difficult provided that you follow some simple guidelines. When planting, make sure that the ground is free from weeds. This may mean using a systemic herbicide. Herbicides of this kind, which are particularly useful for dealing with perennial weeds, enter plants through the leaves and kill them right down to the roots. After dealing with weeds, dig in some additional organic matter if the soil is too light to retain moisture during periods of drought. Add also a slow-release fertilizer, which will ensure that plants get the necessary nutrients during the initial growing stages.

Hedging plants are sold as container-grown specimens, or ball-rooted (with soil held around the roots by burlap) or bare-rooted. Container-grown plants can be planted at most times of the year, although they will need watering during dry spells until they are well established. The expense, however, may well rule out the use of container-grown plants for a hedge of any size. The period for planting ball-rooted and bare-rooted plants – the latter are generally the best value for hedges – depends on whether they are deciduous or evergreen. Plant deciduous species when they are out of leaf, between late autumn and early spring. Evergreen species are best planted either during mid-autumn or mid-spring. Some species, such as Scots pine (*Pinus sylvestris*) and holly (*Ilex aquifolium*), dislike being transplanted at all; in such cases use small plants and make sure that the roots do not dry out. Some people even say that hollies should only be transplanted in late spring; however, with care and the minimum dis-

Solid beech hedges frame a classical vista. The restful green foliage of spring and summer turns coppery brown in autumn and persists throughout the winter, giving a warm tone to the garden. A mature beech hedge 8 feet (2.5m) high can be achieved in about ten years.

turbance to the roots, transplanting can be carried out earlier in the season, when there is likely to be the moisture that is needed to get the plants established.

It is difficult to make general rules about trimming that apply to all kinds of hedges. Steady upward growth is not the only consideration, as unless plenty of lateral growth is encouraged to form, the hedge will be too thin to be effective. With many hedging plants, including beech, privet and Leyland cypress, the best way to achieve this is to trim shoots two or three times in the formative years until growth is dense enough to be maintained with one annual cut, or two in the case of very strong growers. Generally speaking, and particularly with most conifers, the leader should be allowed to grow to the ultimate height of the hedge before it is cut. From the outset, trimming should give the hedge a batter, the sides sloping so that the base is slightly wider than the top. This ensures that the base receives plenty of light and grows strongly.

Most established hedges only require one cut per year. As a rule of thumb, deciduous species should be trimmed in spring before or just as the sap is starting to rise. However, some, such as beech and hornbeam (*Carpinus betulus*), develop very soft growth which needs to be shortened in late spring or early summer if the hedge is to retain its structural quality; but they will retain their leaves longer in the winter if they are trimmed in late summer or early autumn.

To obtain the full benefit of flowering hedges, leave trimming until just after flowering has finished. Evergreen hedges will do best with a late summer trim. *Lonicera nitida*, privet, Leyland cypress and other fast growers that need to be cut several times a year can be trimmed in spring and then again in mid- and late summer.

Even the fastest-growing hedge will take some time to reach the required height. In the interim it may be necessary to provide a temporary screen. One way is to back the plants with trellis panels to the intended height of the hedge. A more solid effect can be achieved by erecting trellis panels both sides of the hedge. This method of boxing in was commonly followed in the 18th century, the plants being trimmed to the size of the enclosure, until it rotted away.

Another technique, described by Nathaniel Lloyd in his classic book *Garden Craftsmanship in Yew and Box*, is to shield the plants with burlap. An extension of this idea is to fix green hessian to green-stained trellis fastened to posts set along the line of the hedge. This temporary screen will protect plants from wind and give the garden privacy.

Evergreens are, as a rule, less hardy than deciduous hedging plants, but there are a few that will normally come through the winter unscathed. Arborvitae (*Thuja occidentalis*), the western hemlock (*Tsuga heterophylla*) and the less commonly used eastern hemlock (*T. canadensis*) are among the best. For less favored areas, where winter temperatures drop very low and for prolonged periods, it is better to choose deciduous species. Quickthorn, *Berberis thunbergii* and *Corylus avellana* are dependable choices. *Prunus cerasifera, P. × cistena* and *P. nigra* are three fast-growing species that are covered with small white flowers in early spring.

A tall evergreen yew hedge runs along either side of a narrow herb garden in which the shapes of topiary box stand out well against the rectilinear background. In late winter (this page, far left) when the shadows are long, the simple ingredients of topiary, circular stone paving and gravel path defined by granite blocks are in themselves pleasing to the eye. In early summer (near left) the young foliage of the golden box lights up the garden and contrasts well with the purple flowerheads of alliums. The garden is much fuller but the pale umbels of angelica and sweet cicely, for example, do not undermine the garden's firm structure.

HEDGES AFTER EIGHT YEARS' GROWTH

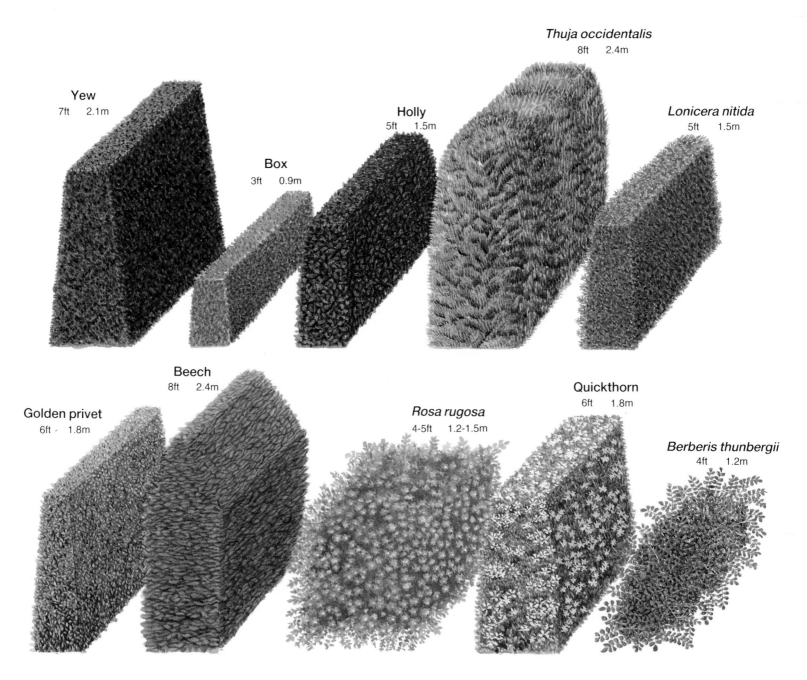

Thuja occidentalis
8ft   2.4m

Yew
7ft   2.1m

Holly
5ft   1.5m

Lonicera nitida
5ft   1.5m

Box
3ft   0.9m

Beech
8ft   2.4m

Golden privet
6ft   1.8m

Quickthorn
6ft   1.8m

Rosa rugosa
4-5ft   1.2-1.5m

Berberis thunbergii
4ft   1.2m

Vigorous but controlled plant growth is the most important factor in making a garden look mature. Unwanted and undisciplined plant growth, on the other hand, can quickly turn a garden into a tangled chaos. Two weeks away on holiday at the height of the growing season is all the time needed for a garden to take on a positively dishevelled appearance. The lawn grows several inches; weeds appear everywhere, pushing their way up among shrubs and perennials, swamping the vegetable garden and colonizing bare soil and paths; where there were flowers there are only deadheads; and the beauty of plants coming into bloom is hidden by rank and untidy growth.

The smaller the garden, the more obvious the effect of a short period of neglect. However, mowing and collecting the grass, pulling the weeds and deadheading the shrubs and perennials will soon put most things right. It is a much more difficult task to restore a garden, particularly a large one, after several years of neglect. Then, typically, the lawn is no more than a field of coarse grasses and other broadleaved weeds. Only strong-growing shrubs and perennials – for example, lilacs and privet, valerian and the old apothecaries' peony – survive among seedlings of trees and shrubs such as ash, sycamore, cotoneaster and buddleja, in an ever-advancing mass of nettles, goose-grass, twitch and thistles. Left to itself, this process of natural regeneration would lead eventually, after decades, to what is called "climactic forest", where the vegetation finds its own balance and the cycle of life and death takes its own course.

The best way to deal with a seriously neglected and overgrown garden is to clear it and start again from scratch. The only plants worth keeping may be a sapling of a good tree, which even in the short term

OVERGROWTH

will give some height to the garden, and a few shrubs that, if capable of rejuvenation, will be useful as fillers in the early years until other plants have grown up. The most efficient way of removing perennial weeds and most tree and shrub seedlings is to use a total herbicide (such as Round-up or Kleen-up), which acts by being translocated through the plant and therefore kills it right down to the roots. It is inactivated as soon as it touches the soil, so does not leave any residues. The time to apply it is when the plants are growing actively and there is plenty of leaf area for the herbicide to penetrate. It must be stressed, however,

that great care must be taken when using any chemical in the garden; if recommended by the manufacturer, protective clothing should be worn.

Drastic pruning will give a new lease of life to many shrubs that have become overgrown through neglect. Although they may be taking up far too much space, these shrubs have probably lost a lot of their vigor, flowering only at the top of the plant above a tangle of dead wood. Severe pruning of deciduous shrubs should be carried out in late autumn or winter rather than in early spring, to allow the plant plenty of time to produce new growth the following season. There will be little or no display from spring-flowering shrubs in the first season after heavy pruning. Evergreen shrubs and conifers should be dealt with in late spring. Any weak shoots should be cut right back to their base and the main stems cut to 2 or 3 feet (60-90cm) from ground level. This treatment usually causes the plant to produce a large number of shoots, most of which will need to be cut down the following winter or spring. Of these, keep three to five to form a framework for the revived shrub. Meanwhile, the plant must be given fertilizers and kept well-watered.

There is an undeniable beauty in gardens teetering on the brink of wild disorder. A garden that reaches this point through neglect will quite rapidly decline into a tangled confusion that can no longer be called a garden. There is, though, a kind of wildness where the precarious balance between order and chaos is maintained by gardening of a very high order. The most enthusiastic protagonists of wild gardening will admit that the woodland garden, for example, where wild plants such as epimediums and trilliums grow harmoniously with primroses and other cultivated perennials, calls for much initial work and constant vigilance.

Page 51: A garden in which the plants have been seeding themselves for years is beginning to blend in with the surrounding countryside.

Left: Only a small pink rose over the wall and heating pipes for a greenhouse indicate that this was once a well-tended garden. Like the house, it has long been abandoned and nature has taken hold, displaying her own beauty.

Right: There is a special charm about gardens teetering on the brink of overmaturity but much work is needed to keep them at this point. Paths quickly disappear under unchecked ornamentals and weeds, and roses that once tumbled gracefully become tangled messes. The pink centranthus in this garden is one perennial that self-seeds freely and holds its own in a neglected garden.

TIME AND PLACE

It is impossible to look at time in the garden without looking also at place: gardening, indeed, may be considered as the point of contact between these two dimensions. The starting point in the creation and re-structuring of any garden is the site itself – the soil conditions, the contours, the distribution of sun and shade, the climate and the microclimate, the existing features that you want to preserve and those that you want to remove. All these factors need to be taken into account in drawing up a plan not only of *what* to do, but also *when* to do it. Unless you plot the timescale of operations realistically, the plan for the garden is incomplete, and the result could be disappointment. When planning major changes, the secret of success is to make an ally of time, so that the garden evolves attractively and fluently, rather than being, at any particular season, all too obviously unfinished. The following section of the book offers some guidelines on the long-term planning of a garden in relation to the potential offered by the site. It includes, in the four garden "compositions", some specific planting suggestions for dry, damp, sunny and shady sites, each composition being chosen for its interest at all times of year. The picture (left) shows a predominantly shady garden, in which euphorbias, irises, pink aquilegias and Welsh poppies make the most of a sunny position in early summer.

LOOKING AT THE SITE

Tempting though it is to make instant decisions about a newly acquired garden, the sensible course is to take sufficient time to discover its potential before undertaking any major work or planting. Whether it is an already established garden or a virgin plot, the first year should be a period of assessment. This does not mean that you should simply sit back. You stand the best chance of making a pleasurable garden if you discover all you can about the ground you are to work with, becoming familiar with everything from the soil to the microclimates the plot encompasses. You can learn a lot from the plants that are already there. There may be scope for some major new planting but the things to concentrate on initially are annuals or crops of vegetables. You may be able to manage no more than a small sunny patch but even this will give encouragement, and from it you will learn about the unique conditions of your garden. By growing some plants you will help to keep down weeds, which will have to be eradicated in any case, either by physical removal or by spraying with a herbicide during the growing season. If perennial weeds are not eradicated before permanent planting goes in, they can turn the pleasant art of gardening into a nightmare.

During the initial year of assessment one of the first points to establish is the nature of the soil. When you know whether it is acid, alkaline or neutral you can begin to look through catalogs with the serious intention of planting your garden. But you need to know, too, whether the soil is fast-draining, moisture-retentive or even boggy. The quicker-draining soils warm up early in the spring, encouraging plant growth. Moisture-retentive soils warm up slowly but plants obtain the benefit during long hot spells in summer. There are plants for every type of soil but almost all soils can be improved to allow a fairly broad range of plants to be grown. Boggy ground is especially limiting, and it is almost certainly worth making a major effort to improve poor drainage.

Although from the outset you may know the general climate of the area in which your garden lies, it will take a full year to appreciate the features of the garden's microclimate. The way sun reaches different areas of the garden will change with the seasons. In summer deciduous trees may cast shade that was quite unexpected in winter. You will have a chance, too, to discover the direction of the prevailing wind and the sunny warm corners that are miraculously sheltered. Wind and frost are particularly damaging to plants; on the basis of your survey throughout a year you may well think it worth planting hedges to give protection to cold and exposed parts of the garden.

The year of assessment will also give you an opportunity to decide how best to use the garden as an outdoor room and as a place in which to relax. Is the fact that neighbors can see in of no great concern, or do you want to plant or build to engineer privacy? The size, shape and exposure of the site will govern how you arrange areas for sitting out to catch the sun or, in hot countries, to benefit from shade. There may also be more fundamental structural decisions to make on the basis of your assessment. On a steeply sloping site you may decide that terracing is essential. Soil-moving is best done in early or late winter when there is little else to do, and the ground is not frozen.

A garden does not exist in isolation. It is almost invariably the adjunct of a house, which is itself set in a landscape or townscape. The way the garden is designed ought to take its companion architecture into account and also the general surroundings. You may be lucky enough to have something attractive outside the garden, such as a church spire, to incorporate as a borrowed view in the design. It is much more likely, however, that the design will have to hide unsightly features, some of which may not show until trees are bare of leaves in the autumn.

With the information you glean over a year you will be able to plan confidently, although it will not always be easy to balance the competing claims for the prime sunny and sheltered parts of the garden. In making what can sometimes be difficult choices it will help enormously if you can draw on the experience of others – not only distinguished writers such as Christopher Lloyd on meadow gardening, Rosemary Verey on the garden in winter or Gertrude Jekyll on color, but also friends and neighbors. If possible, you should talk to garden owners, for they too will have encountered a wide range of problems, and the ways in which they have overcome them may help you deal with the challenges posed by your own garden.

Opposite, above: The provision of shelter is one of the first requirements on an exposed site. Hedges filter wind, breaking its force without creating areas of turbulence as solid barriers do. In this windswept garden, young deciduous trees and a yew hedge have recently been planted to give shelter in the future.

Left: The planning of a garden must be related to the specific requirements of the site. One of the main advantages of this site is the pretty view it offers across fields. What also had to be taken into account in the design is the garden's long thin shape, sloping down to a river that floods regularly. Furthermore, to one side, out of this picture, there is a power station. The main view has been successfully retained by keeping the central axis clear of plants. Trees help to obscure the power station and the varying depth of planting along the side boundaries has helped camouflage the narrowness of the site. A change in the surfacing helps break up the space, as do steps introduced in the paved area between two lawns. One benefit of such a narrowly chaneled view is that it can be framed both sides with attractive garden plants.

DRAWING UP THE PLAN

Even during the early stages when a site is being assessed, it is worth making rough plans of the garden you think you would like. There is no single design solution to any site, but among the many options there will be one at least that suits your tastes, needs and free time and is within your financial resources. The same design may not suit in five or six years, for example when children have grown up, and certainly in making rough drawings it is worth considering how the garden might evolve. The use of certain areas might be altered, the planting changed and features added. The older gardener, however, may simply want to move towards a design that requires less maintenance, with large areas devoted to ground cover.

Whatever these more distant prospects, when making a plan for the medium-term future it may help to have a theme in mind to give direction and coherence to the design. You might, for instance, aim for a cottage-garden effect or you might prefer a more formal layout, in which loose planting is contained by clipped evergreens. On the other hand, your principal theme may be defined by the use of a dominant color against which to play other colors throughout the seasons.

It is of crucial importance that you bear in mind the maintenance program necessary for the garden that you are designing. There is no point in devoting a large area to fruit and vegetables if it is unlikely that you can keep up with what is generally labor-intensive gardening. The time that it will take to implement the plan and carry out the maintenance program over the next

Opposite and left: There may be times when you want to transform the look of your garden while retaining some of its best features. Before making changes you should first draw a ground plan of the site and on this you can mark your proposed scheme. The transformation from informal cottage garden to formal layout shown in these two photographs was carried through in just under a year, though the preliminary planning was done well in advance. The sundial has been emphasized as the focal point of a strongly symmetrical arrangement in which brick-edged gravel paths have replaced the grass of the less formal garden. The four *Prunus cerasifera* 'Pissardii' are an integral part of the new scheme, standing out against the fast-growing windbreak of *Populus tremula*.

point you need to have a ground plan drawn to scale. The ground plan should have marked on it all existing features, also in true scale. If there are features outside the garden that are significant to the design, these should also be marked on the ground plan as they are easily forgotten in your enthusiasm for a cherished design. If these are not marked in, you may find the main vista of your design lining up unintentionally on a telegraph pole – as has happened to me – or even something less attractive.

If your site is steeply sloping or very irregular it will almost certainly be worth drawing it to scale in cross section. This is essential if you are going to undertake any major terracing, for you need to check that retaining walls are solid enough for their height and have adequate footings.

It pays to go over the site very carefully with the ground plan and the superimposed design in your hand, as you may well find that there is room for revision. Check that where you want to separate one area of the garden from another you have allowed for the right sort of demarcation. You might use a hedge, a pergola or some other vertical barrier, or you may find that a more subtle effect is adequate, using, for example, a change of level or simply a change of surface material. It is especially important to check the position of focal points and the lines of any vistas that include them, bearing in mind the views from doors and windows (ground floor and above). Before committing yourself to a design, make sure that you are satisfied with the proportion of borders to lawn and hard surfaces, and that paths are wide enough to take the traffic they will have to carry. If you find that your lawn has been sited in a dank area under trees, think again, because a good lawn needs a sunny, well-drained position.

two to five years should be an essential element in your calculations.

Your site may be a featureless rectangle attached to a new house, a derelict site that has never been developed or an existing garden with hard paths, an old shed, shrubs, hedges and borders (perhaps all in a poor state); but whatever your starting

Left, above: Before building steps and retaining walls, draw a plan of your site in cross-section. As well as being functional, steps can be very decorative. These granite treads have been well integrated into the garden, the toadflax growing in the cracks and red and white valerian smothering the sides, enhancing the impression of established maturity. It would take two or three years to achieve this effect.

Left, below: The dividers and screens that give shelter and create intimacy in a garden should be included in the plan. For all its elegance, this trellis screen is not a flimsy structure. It makes a bold architectural statement, here emphasized by the pattern of its cast shadows on the frozen ground; and yet it allows glimpses of other parts of the garden and its arched doorway is an invitation to explore further.

PLANNING THE TIMESCALE

To implement the design you have drawn up needs a plan of its own, with a realistic timescale built in. There are many factors to take into account. For the work envisaged you must calculate what time and money are necessary, and what will be available over a given period. The order in which jobs are to be tackled needs to be sorted out, and you need to identify sources for materials and plants.

If you have a small garden, it may be possible to achieve all the construction and planting in one year. But, taking all factors into account, not least the vagaries of the weather, even a small town garden is likely to take more than a year. Err on the generous side when planning, making each stage easy enough to achieve without mistakes, and without the risk of falling discouragingly behind schedule. In any case, be sufficiently flexible to allow adjustments to the plan as you go along. This is particularly important with a large design where the implementation and maintenance plan may extend over several years.

It is, of course, best to establish the hard structure first, including walls, paved areas and paths, steps, raised beds and water features. The next phase can include the laying of lawns and the planting of trees and hedges. This is probably the best stage, too, for building structures such as summer houses and pergolas. The detailed planting comes last, and the way you clothe the garden with shrubs, climbing plants, ground cover, herbaceous perennials, bulbs, annuals, herbs, vegetables and fruit crops can be refined over many years. The way you ornament the garden with statues, sculpture or containers can also be adjusted over a long period. You may find it helpful to use an attractive plant in a container to mark a focal point until a more substantial ornament is available or affordable.

Page 61: An essential part of planning is assessing the time it will take to implement a design in the light of the resources available. Starting from scratch it would take only about two years to achieve the mature effect of the small paved garden illustrated, provided that there was some professional help in laying the hard surfaces. Earth works, leveling and terracing preparatory to the construction of the retaining walls, steps and paving should be the first things to be dealt with. Paint walls and erect trellis work before planting climbers. The main planting is the last stage before positioning furniture.

Right: The work involved in constructing large features such as rock gardens and ponds can be considerable, and you should postpone starting until you know that you have a reasonable period of free time available. Pictured here is a rock garden planted seven years before the photograph was taken. The planting has been designed to peak in spring and early summer, before the owner's annual vacation; the margins of the pond are planted with irises, kingcups, mimulus and primulas.

Far right: The process of maturing continues long after the planned implementation of a garden scheme, although after a certain point the changes are less marked. In a mature garden such as this there is plenty of scope for making changes to much of the planting but to take out or replace trees and shrubs would be a major undertaking. Dominant here are the rounded slow-growing conifer *Chamaecyparis lawsoniana* 'Fletcheri', kept in shape by pruning back hard in late summer. Arching over the top is a slow-growing *Cornus controversa* 'Variegata', which like many other members of the genus has red twigs in winter. The superb ground cover in this garden is a key factor in keeping down maintenance.

After you have spent some time working in the garden, you will get a realistic idea of the speed at which you can proceed. Remember that as soon as you have finished one area, that area will now have to be maintained: the vegetables will need watering, a young hedge will need weeding, climbers will have to be trained, shrubs pruned and grass cut. All these tasks take time out of your schedule and need to be built into the general plan. For these reasons you will find that the best time to undertake major works is from late autumn to early spring, the period when growth is at a minimum. Often, however, jobs have to be done when time is available. You may find, for example, that the only opportunity for digging out a pond is during a week of your summer vacation. The more you do, the more experience and skills you acquire, and jobs begin to take less time.

Obtaining materials just when you want them can often be a problem, either because they are not available or because your funds are not adequate. You may have acquired just the right number of columns to make a small temple which is going to be the main focal point of the garden but have not yet solved the problem of roofing it within your budget. It is better to take all the time that is needed to achieve the desired effect – there will always be plenty of other things to do in the meantime.

Whether you do all the construction yourself or employ someone to do it, pay attention to detail and finish. It is particularly important to make sure that all paving is properly laid. If you are putting down gravel, lay it on a plastic sheet to prevent weeds growing through; in the long term this will save a lot of time.

In more formal parts of the garden, steps look better if they are nosed, that is with a projecting lip. Whatever part of the garden they are in, they must be safe to use and comfortable to ascend. It is important that walls should be well pointed before any planting is done, as work carried out subsequently will involve trampling over beds and detaching climbers, which is both time-consuming and detrimental to the growth of plants.

All this is straightforward when starting with a new, featureless site, but making major alterations to an existing garden presents a different range of problems. One way is to clear the site before you start, but such a drastic approach has its disadvantages. The time, labor and funds necessary may simply not be available. Furthermore, the site will look very raw and new for a few years.

My advice is to select existing elements to help you in developing the new design of the garden. For example, an old shed will be useful in early years to house tools until such time as it can be rebuilt, perhaps in a more suitable position. Provided that they are not so close that they create shade or competition, existing hedges are useful on exposed sites to protect young plants – particularly those set out to screen and separate new sections of the garden. An overgrown border or any other area that accumulates weeds should perhaps be grassed down for easy maintenance, but I would always recommend keeping at least a small area under cultivation. This will provide the satisfaction of a garden in miniature, and give encouragement as you contemplate the manifold tasks ahead.

COMPOSITION FOR A DAMP SITE

Few of us have the good fortune to have a natural stream in our garden, but it is possible without too much trouble to create a pool by excavating a hole and lining it with a heavy-gauge plastic liner. Plants that thrive on a plentiful supply of water and are hardy enough to withstand the winter in wet conditions can then be grown all around the margins of the pool. The farther away from the pool and the sunnier the site, the drier the conditions.

The most water-retentive soils are those rich in organic matter. These soils tend to be acidic. The addition of peat or leaf-mold will help to create the right conditions.

The site illustrated here is two banks of a natural stream shaded by a large sycamore, with a hedgerow on the other side. It receives most sun in the evening. These conditions ensure that the soil remains moist and cool throughout the growing season.

The greatest show of color is in late spring and early summer when the balance between temperature and moisture levels is at its optimum. For the rest of the season, foliage provides a rich tapestry of form and color enhanced in autumn by the fruits in the hedgerow.

A

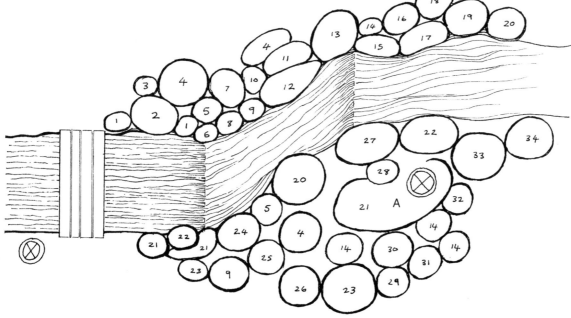

A Sycamore (*Acer pseudoplatanus*)
1 *Lythrum salicaria*
2 *Brunnera* 'Langtrees'
3 *Iris foetidissima*
4 *Pulmonaria saccharata*
5 *Alchemilla mollis*
6 *Iris pseudacorus*
7 *Polygonatum multiflorum*
8 *Pulmonaria* 'Lewis Palmer'
9 *Scrophularia aquatica*
10 *Chaerophyllum hirsutum*
11 *Primula denticulata*
12 *Ajuga* 'Tortoiseshell'
13 *Polygonum amplexicaule*
   'Atrosanguineum'   14 *Hosta*
15 *Caltha polypetala*
16 *Lamium* 'White Nancy'
17 *Iris pseudacorus* 'Variegata'
18 *Geum aquaticum*
19 *Carex stricta* 'Bowles Golden'
20 *Rheum palmatum*
21 *Lamium maculatum* 'Roseum'
22 *Astilbe*
23 *Polemonium foliosissimum*
24 *Hosta* 'Thomas Hogg'
25 *Veronica* 'Hidcote Pink'
26 *Salix fargesii*
27 *Astrantia maxima*
28 *Thalictrum aquilegifolium*
29 *Hosta* 'Frances Williams'
30 *Sanguisorba magnifica*
31 *Artemisia vulgaris* 'Variegata'
32 *Veronica spicata*
33 *Philadelphus coronarius* 'Aureus'
34 *Rosa spinosissima* 'Heather Muir'

B

C

A *Early spring: The daffodils are in flower, and the perennials just emerging.*
B *Late spring: The stream bank is covered in flowering perennials.*
C *Mid-summer: The vegetation has reached its height. Hosta leaves, sword-shaped iris leaves and the huge* Rheum palmatum *leaves are among the most prominent.*
D *Early autumn: Russets of dying vegetation last until the frosts.*

D

COMPOSITION FOR A DRY SITE

A dry garden is perhaps the most difficult to cope with, because the lack of water inevitably inhibits growth. However, as with all other situations, there are plants that will thrive. The ones to look out for are those from areas of low rainfall, such as the Mediterranean region, and parts of Central Asia, South Africa and America where the main precipitation is from late autumn to spring and the summers are periods of great drought.

The garden illustrated here is part of the larger garden created by the distinguished English plantswoman and writer Beth Chatto, which she began just over 30 years ago. The soil in this part of the garden is sand and gravel that has been enriched over the years with compost and leaf-mold. The slope receives the sun for most of the day and in summer gets a real baking.

The planting plan shows a detail of the garden. The framework, which has now reached maturity, includes such tall evergreens as *Taxus baccata* 'Fastigiata' and *Chamaecyparis lawsoniana* 'Ellwoodii' (27). There are also large shrubs of *Cytisus battandieri* (7), *Erica arborea* (29) and *Cistus ladanifer*.

Many of the ground-cover plants and smaller shrubs – including sages (25), lavender (28), santolinas (12), thymes (32) – are aromatic.

A Early spring: The evergreen Euphorbia characias wulfenii *(4) has biennial stems with grey-green leaves the first year and yellow-green blooms the second.*
B Late spring: At the end of the gravel path a tall Paulownia tomentosa *contrasts sharply with the upright evergreen silhouette of an Irish yew (*Taxus baccata *'Fastigiata').*
C Summer: The evergreen mound of Viburnum davidii *is partially shaded by a large holly (*Ilex*) which serves as a backdrop to white delphiniums. In the heart of the dry garden the yellow spires of* Verbascum chaixii *are complemented by the paler yellow daisy flowers of* Anthemis tinctoria *'E.C. Buxton' (22).*
D Autumn: The late-flowering Nerine bowdenii *(16) introduces color among the permanent grays and greens.*

A

B

C

D

1 *Verbascum pulverulentum*	17 *Euphorbia myrsinites*
2 *Artemisia arborescens*	18 *Stachys olympica*
3 *Digitalis purpurea*	19 *Stachys lanata*
4 *Euphorbia characias wulfenii*	20 *Grindelia chiloensis*
5 *Sedum* 'Ruby Glow'	21 *Veronica perfoliata*
6 *Dorycnium hirsutum*	22 *Anthemis tinctoria* 'E.C. Buxton'
7 *Cytisus battandieri*	23 *Hebe*
8 Red tulips	24 *Yucca*
9 *Armeria* 'Dusseldorf Pink'	25 *Salvia officinalis* 'Purpurascens'
10 *Molinia caerulea* 'Variegata'	26 *Penstemon menziesii*
11 *Laurus nobilis*	27 *Chamaecyparis lawsoniana* 'Ellwoodii'
12 *Santolina chamaecyparissus*	28 *Lavandula* 'Munstead Blue'
13 *Allium aflatunense*	29 *Erica arborea*
14 *Sedum*	30 *Fritillaria imperialis*
15 *Ballota pseudodictamnus*	31 *Gaura lindheimeri*
16 *Nerine bowdenii*	32 *Thymus* 'Pink Chintz'

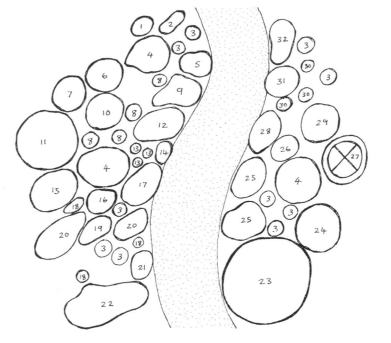

COMPOSITION FOR A SUNNY SITE

Most gardens have at least one part that receives the sun for most of the day. A border for sun-loving plants is easily created, as there are so many to choose from.

One of the advantages of many sunny sites is that the soil warms up quickly in spring, and consequently plants start into growth early. However, the soil very often dries out quickly in summer, and the result can be stunted growth or flagging plants. A good mulch in spring is particularly valuable for conserving moisture in sunny borders.

The border illustrated here was developed over several years (see pp. 14-15), with plants continually added or removed to achieve the most rewarding effect. It benefits from the protection and additional warmth of an old wall, which provides a beautiful backdrop to the design.

The sea of self-sown forget-me-nots in spring (A) announces the blue theme that is taken up in summer (B). In the interim, from spring to early summer, tulips and other bulbs provide a changing display of color. The bold heads of a euphorbia (23) make the most enduring display throughout the seasons.

A

A Late spring: In the second half of the season, tulips such as 'Gold Medal' (20), 'Black Swan' (13), the pink 'Angélique' (5) and the purple 'Greuze' (15) make a vivid display.
B Summer: Alliums (11), cranesbills (10, 16 and 22), Iris sibirica (17) and the rugosa rose 'Roseraie de l'Haÿ' (3) establish a predominantly purple and blue theme.
C Autumn: The foliage of the rose is turning to yellow, and some striking ornamental cabbages, treated as infilling annuals, have reached their peak.
D Winter: As winter draws to a close the most conspicuous plants are Erysimum *'Bowles' Mauve' (14) and* Euphorbia characias wulfenii *(23).*

B

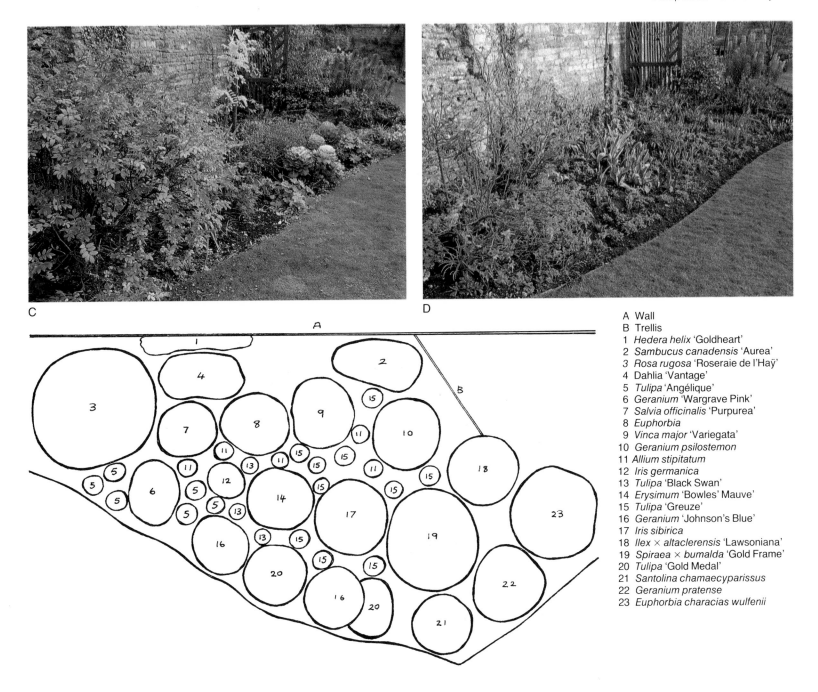

C

D

A Wall
B Trellis
1 *Hedera helix* 'Goldheart'
2 *Sambucus canadensis* 'Aurea'
3 *Rosa rugosa* 'Roseraie de l'Haÿ'
4 Dahlia 'Vantage'
5 *Tulipa* 'Angélique'
6 *Geranium* 'Wargrave Pink'
7 *Salvia officinalis* 'Purpurea'
8 *Euphorbia*
9 *Vinca major* 'Variegata'
10 *Geranium psilostemon*
11 *Allium stipitatum*
12 *Iris germanica*
13 *Tulipa* 'Black Swan'
14 *Erysimum* 'Bowles' Mauve'
15 *Tulipa* 'Greuze'
16 *Geranium* 'Johnson's Blue'
17 *Iris sibirica*
18 *Ilex × altaclerensis* 'Lawsoniana'
19 *Spiraea × bumalda* 'Gold Frame'
20 *Tulipa* 'Gold Medal'
21 *Santolina chamaecyparissus*
22 *Geranium pratense*
23 *Euphorbia characias wulfenii*

COMPOSITION FOR A SHADY SITE

Many gardeners look with despair on shaded parts of the garden. However, there are many plants that thrive in light or even deep shade, and these can be used to create borders that combine handsome foliage and flowers. Natural woodlanders are among the most suitable. Many – daffodils (5), hellebores (9), primroses (20), and snowdrops (21) – flower in winter or spring, when the leaf canopy is thin, and when light penetrates to the ground. Other woodlanders, including aquilegias (12) and violas (13), carry the season through when the canopy has filled out.

Even plants such as roses that are generally thought of as sun-lovers can perform well in part shade, although they may not flower as freely as they would in a more open position.

Most shady borders have cool moist soil, conditions suiting a wide range of plants. Even for dry shady areas, the most difficult sites in the garden, there are tough plants that will survive and prosper, although they may be slow to establish themselves.

The garden illustrated here is shaded by a tall tulip tree, although the lower branches have been pruned to let in enough light to allow a wide range of plants to be grown.

A

1 *Jasminum revolutum*
2 *Digitalis purpurea*
3 *Meconopsis cambrica*
4 *Stephanandra tanakae*
5 *Narcissi*
6 *Pulmonaria saccharata*
7 *Hyacinthoides non-scripta*
8 *Tulipa* 'Holland's Glory'
9 *Helleborus orientalis*
10 *Brunnera macrophylla*
11 *Hemerocallis* 'Flore Pleno' ('Kwanso')
12 *Aquilegia*
13 *Viola cornuta*
14 Roses
15 *Myosotis*
16 *Hebe*
17 Border pinks
18 *Rosa* 'Alex's Red'
19 *Nepeta* × *faassenii*
20 *Primula vulgaris*
21 *Galanthus nivalis*

B

C

D

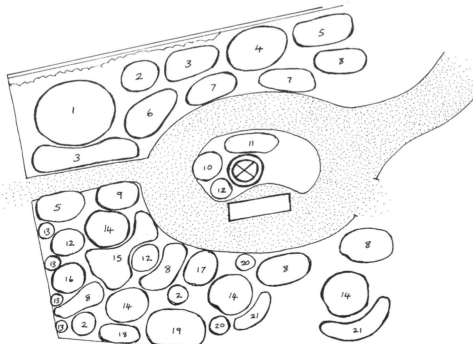

A *Late spring: A few flowers, including forget-me-nots (15) and aquilegias (12), bridge the gap between the spring and summer flushes.*

B *Summer: At the edge of a shady bed two roses obtain enough sunlight to flower freely. Tall foxgloves (2) are already over but violas (13) flower freely in the shade.*

C *Autumn: A red bloom of the rose 'Alex's Red' stands out prominently against the fallen butter-yellow leaves of the tulip tree.*

D *Mid-spring: Tulips (8) and forget-me-nots (15) have taken over from the early-season woodland plants such as snowdrops and hellebores.*

SHORTCUTS TO MATURITY

The appeal of a mature garden is almost universal. Plants in their prime leave scarcely a patch of bare earth, and stems trailing here and there will break up any rigid formality in the design. In time, all the man-made features become mellow, showing none of the disconcerting rawness of new walls and paths, fresh woodwork, shining sculpture, or pristine pots and containers. In brief, a mature garden seems to belong as much to the past as to the present, part of a continuous tradition that nearly all cultures value. It is often surprising how quickly a garden can take on a mature appearance, and nothing contributes more to this than healthy plant growth encouraged by good cultivation. There are, however, a number of ways by which the maturing process can be accelerated so that the garden quickly takes on the patina of age.

One obvious way is to begin with a design inspired by gardens of the past. A pattern of knots, that is small beds surrounded by clipped box or other low hedging, a chamomile lawn and a simple fountain placed centrally might suggest a medieval garden. The formal manner of the 17th century might be captured with an intricate parterre combined with long straight paths and vistas. A garden in the spirit of the 19th century could include shrubberies, meandering paths and colorful bedding. To give these gardens an authentic character the plants need to be appropriate to the chosen period. In a "medieval garden" the plants should include medicinal herbs, many of which are the wild forms of plants since hybridized to make our modern garden plants. The most typical plants of late 17th-century gardens were the so-called "greens". These were evergreen plants such as laurustinus (*Viburnum tinus*), phillyrea (*Phillyrea angustifolia*), alaternus (*Rhamnus alaternus*

Opposite and above: **The patina of marble and moss- and lichen-covered stone help to convey an impression of maturity. In the garden, opposite, the cherry has been pruned to restrict its spread, so that it takes on the appearance of a gnarled old tree; generous planting also helps.**

angustifolia), pyracantha (*Pyracantha coccinea*), myrtle (*Myrtus communis*), bay (*Laurus nobilis*) and yew (*Taxus baccata*). They were usually tightly clipped into geometric shapes (there were published pattern books to follow); as many were tender, they were often grown in pots and brought in for the winter. Plants for a shrubbery in the 19th-century manner could include spotted laurel (*Aucuba japonica*), mock orange (*Philadelphus tomentosus*) and a rhododendron (for example, *Rh. campanulatum*) shading ferns and ivy. For a patterned bedding scheme the choice could include bright geraniums (*Pelargonium*), french marigolds (*Tagetes erecta*), ageratum and salvias.

Ornaments and features appropriate to the period you have chosen can complement the planting. Heraldic beasts, a thyme seat and an arcade of rustic wood would suit a "medieval garden". Obelisks, classical benches and simple trelliswork would be in keeping with the formal tone of the 17th century; a more ambitious feature to add would be a mount, or mound (sometimes referred to as a tump). Intricate stone urns, rustic furniture and wrought-iron arbors were all familiar features in 19th-century gardens.

Even when you are not aiming for a precise period style, a mature effect can be achieved only if care is taken in the choice of materials. Plastic seats, pots and ornaments, however well molded, will never give an impression of substance and, rather than weather and improve with age, they will tend to deteriorate or when cleaned will look too new. Materials with smooth surfaces – marble, glass, gilded and painted surfaces – generally do not acquire a patina over time. Most modern types of paint tend to peel and look shabby after several years, but the microporous paints and stains which are now available weather over the years in a more attractive manner.

Many other materials used in garden ornament – among them stone, concrete, bronze, copper, lead, terracotta and unpainted hardwood – age very appealingly. Some manufacturers of reconstituted stone make a strong point of the way in which the pores in their materials retain water and encourage the growth of moss and lichens. Adding a nutrient will accelerate such growth. You can do this by pouring or painting on natural or artificial manure mixed with water, with a dash of dishwashing liquid as a wetting agent. Sour milk or yogurt are suitable alternatives, more easily obtained in most homes. Adding ordinary soil to the mixture will speed up the darkening of pores and reduce the hardness of a new plant pot or sculpture. Stone and concrete ornaments placed in the shade of trees where they will catch drips will quickly acquire a coating of moss and lichens.

Paved areas and paths are included in almost every garden design, and well-chosen materials for these will do much to give a garden a mature look. Old paving stones and bricks are ideal. The eye immediately detects modern concrete paving slabs because they are too flat and regular in shape. Their outlines can be softened to some extent by encouraging plants to spill over the edge of beds or by introducing small plants between the cracks and allowing them to self-seed. Although they require more maintenance, gravel paths, even when newly laid, are more in keeping with the look of an established garden than concrete or black top. However, unless held in by an edging, gravel will spread. Modern plastic or galvanised edging may serve the purpose but will never mellow, so it is better to use a simple wood edging. Other possibilities are

reclaimed or reproduction 19th-century tile edging.

Traditional gardens often include metal objects. Bronze or copper items turn green with copper salts as they weather. This process can be induced by the use of chemicals. Muriatic acid, for example, will produce an immediate effect; some care should be taken in applying the acid to achieve a natural effect. A patina should be mottled so that it breaks up the original hard outline of an object, making it blend more convincingly with its natural surroundings. In the 16th and 17th centuries, lead statuary was often painted, and in some restorations of old gardens the sculpture, which had been weathered lead for many years, has been restored to its original painted state. This is one way to cover the effects of major repairs. The same can be done with modern reproduction statuary in less costly materials.

Unpainted hardwoods such as oak and elm weather to a light grey in a fairly short time when exposed to the elements. The wood can be left untreated for a year or two, but then a preservative should be applied to arrest any decay that has set in. The wood can be darkened and water-proofed by the use of boiled or raw linseed oil (the boiled oil produces a darker color). Another way to preserve old hardwood is to spray on a proprietary wax after treatment with a wood preservative. Softwoods will need some form of treatment from the beginning, and a wide range of colored preservatives is available for them. Green, gray and blue are colors that blend in well with a garden setting.

Second-hand materials, now available from specialist suppliers, can give built structures an authentically aged appearance. New cement joints and additional new materials can be toned down by painting over with the nutrient solutions

mentioned earlier. Of course, unless the garden features suit the mood of their setting, their awkwardness will contradict the impression of maturity you want to create. A grotto, for example, can make a virtue of shade, brightening it with the reflection of trickling water, but would look out of place in an exposed position.

There is a great deal of pleasure to be had in tracking down a particular style of ornament. A piece chosen with discrimination can do much to lend the garden a mature distinction. The ornament will be all

the more convincing if the subject is suited to its setting. A Neptune for a water garden, sheaves of corn or baskets of fruit in a country garden, obelisks in a formal architectural setting, large oil jars in a courtyard. At one time nearly every English and American colonial garden boasted a sundial, and in an open, sunny position such an ornament can still be attractive and suggest a continuity with the past.

The mottoes that sundials carry are an appealing feature, but these need not be the only inscriptions decorating a garden. Poetic verses, epitaphs or reminders of other places or times inscribed on stone or metal plaques can be set in walls, over doors, on the ground or raised on plinths, perhaps leading on from one part of the garden to another.

Left, top: Well-shaped topiary and stone walls always give the impression that a garden has been established for years.
Left, bottom: This classical 18th-century carved stone basket of fruit, probably of French origin, has acquired a rich patina of age, moss having colonized its intricate surface. Modern reproductions in porous cast-stone hold water and weather quickly, particularly if kept under the shade of trees.
Below: In a shady corner the outstanding camellia 'Donation' looks particularly striking in an old copper tub that has acquired a green patina. The wooden bench beside it is well weathered and the stone paving has been invaded by moss.

A collection of pot-grown plants can provide a whole sequence of compositions throughout the seasons. Laburnums, flowering in late spring, are the main feature of this stylish arrangement around an old water jar. The yellow contrasts particularly effectively with the gray wall. Later in the year the same color theme could perhaps be continued by pot-grown lilies. An arrangement of french or african marigolds would be more commonplace but, by way of compensation, would enjoy a longer season – summer to early autumn.

TIMELY SOLUTIONS

Even when you know you are not going to live in a particular house for any length of time, you will still want a garden that looks attractive and gives pleasure. The obvious course is to plant in a way that will give satisfaction in the short term. On the other hand, if you are likely to have your garden for a long period, perhaps the rest of your life, the aim of your main planting will be to create a mature effect in the long term; so that for several years the garden will look rather thin and unfinished unless you find ways of filling the gaps. Both these situations pose an interesting challenge – that of providing interest without undue loss of time – to which there are a number of solutions, ranging from the planting of semi-mature stock to the use of fast-growing plants, such as annuals, vegetables and some climbers.

BUYING TIME

Most trees and shrubs sold by nurseries and garden centres are young stock, and for a year or two they do not make much impact in the garden. It is possible, though, to buy more mature plants that have been grown on in the nursery for several years, and these can be very useful for filling in the garden and giving it a coherent structure. The sort of thing available includes cones and standards of box and holly and, for greater height, heavy nursery stock standards, which can measure from 8 to 13 feet (2.4-4m), of almost anything from forest conifers to flowering cherries. It is even possible to buy ready-trained fan or espalier fruit trees 6 feet (1.8m) high. From the outset these are impressive planted against a wall or as a screen, tied to wires that are fixed between steel posts.

Plants with some age are inevitably expensive, so it is important to get sound stock. It may be worth going to a nursery to choose a well-proportioned healthy specimen during the growing season. I like to think of plants such as these as a way of "buying time", but it is not just a simple matter of paying more for a more mature plant. The older the plant, the more difficult it is to transplant, and therefore the more care must be taken when doing so. However well treated, older trees and shrubs that have had their roots severed during lifting in the nursery will take two or more years to settle down before making any significant growth.

Large containerized plants are often available, and these have the advantage that they can be planted at any time of the year. Bare-rooted plants that are bought or delivered in winter must be unwrapped and planted immediately so that the roots do not dry out or freeze. If the site you have chosen is temporarily too wet or the soil too hard, heel the plants in, adding sand and peat to the soil. In exposed positions protect new stock from wind by means of a burlap screen. The planting hole should be large enough to accommodate the roots comfortably when they are spread out, giving the tree or shrub the maximum chance of getting plenty of water and nutrients, and a solid anchorage. The soil, to which a slow-release fertilizer should be added, needs to be carefully worked in among the roots; the fertilizer will begin to act when the tree needs it in the spring. A short stake, treated against rot, driven firmly into the base of the planting pit will provide stability while the plant becomes established. The stake need only extend to

a quarter or a third of the height of the plant and can be taken out after two or three years. Tie the tree or shrub to the stake securely with a good-quality tie, neither too tight nor too slack, and check it from time to time for effectiveness.

A less expensive alternative to buying semi-mature trees and shrubs is to obtain young stock of very fast-growing kinds such as the hybrid poplar *Populus* 'Robusta' or one of the birches, for example *Betula pendula* or *B. papyrifera*. If planted as 3 to 5-foot (90-150cm) whips, they will soon catch up with any larger tree and be very showy. Even if poplars are used as a nurse to a beech, say, they will need their lower branches pruned to give the beech space and light; and they should be felled after ten or fifteen years. I have experience of this in a previous garden. We appreciated the presence of the poplars, which grew very quickly and gave the young garden an air of maturity, but we were very glad to leave the job of felling them to our successor.

At a more modest level you could buy time by purchasing young bedding plants and vegetables – a point that is taken up in the next chapter.

One other course you might consider to give a garden an established look quickly is to lay a lawn using bought turf. Turf is expensive, but it is worth going to a reputable supplier, as much that is sold is of poor quality. The best time to lay turf is the autumn and winter, and for a good result the ground must be thoroughly prepared before the turves are laid. After rolling and brushing to lift the flattened grass, the lawn will look surprisingly presentable, although it will not be truly established until spring. An area of green combined with instant architectural features of trelliswork can make a very convincing start to a garden.

Opposite page: Large nursery-grown stock can make an instant impact in the garden, although younger plants will often overtake them in a few years. A particularly heavy standard specimen of sweetgum (*Liquidambar styraciflua*) has been lifted and the roots balled and wrapped ready for shipping.

Left: Many trees, including maples and flowering cherries, are widely available as standards, and these give instant height to a garden. The standard maple here unfurling its leaves in the spring will afford a canopy to perennials and low-growing shrubs. An upright specimen of juniper, one of many conifers that can be bought as well-grown plants, makes a vertical accent, especially valuable in the winter.

Above: Conifers are particularly useful for giving the garden a clothed look through the seasons. Many are slow-growing but, if well-developed plants are bought and skillfully grouped, they create an impression of established durability.

BRIEF LIVES

Plants that reach maturity in one or at most two years, flowering, setting seed and then dying, are among the most useful for creating quick effects in the garden. The ornamentals include annuals, biennials and a few tender perennials that in temperate gardens are grown as annuals. Most vegetables are also short-lived; although the primary reason for growing them may be their culinary value, they can make wonderfully decorative gardens on their own or combined with ornamentals.

Most short-lived plants, whether vegetables or ornamentals, are easily raised from seed, and by sowing batches in succession it is possible to extend the flowering and cropping season over several months.

For really speedy results the answer is to buy young plants – for example, summer bedding plants and vegetables in the spring. Garden centers often have young stock available early in the season, but half-hardy plants, before being put into the open garden, must be hardened off while there is still a risk of frosts.

Bedding schemes on the grand scale, with flowers massed for bold color effects, are now rarely seen except in a few public parks. But there is scope even in the small garden for a modest version of this 19th-century practice. Some of the plants that were popular more than a century ago – lobelias, pelargoniums, petunias, salvias and verbenas – are still among the most reliable for giving a sustained display of flower power. Others that flower freely over a long period include begonias, heliotrope, impatiens and matricaria. The best effects with massed color are generally achieved when the planting is confined to beds of

Many plants make up for their short lives by the spread of their growth and by providing foliage, flowers and fruit in great abundance. Those that are useful are very often consigned to the vegetable garden, although they can be highly ornamental. The conventional ornamentals are commonly used in annual bedding schemes or as fillers, serving as temporary planting while perennials and shrubs reach maturity. There are, however, more imaginative ways to use short-lived plants, and one of the most attractive is in schemes that combine vegetables and ornamentals. The sweet peas and squashes that in this garden have been trained over arches could be replaced in subsequent years by other annual climbers, including runner beans, *Thunbergia alata* or *Tropaeolum peregrinum*.

regular geometric shape within a formal layout.

A simple scheme that would give color throughout much of the year might consist of winter pansies, perhaps interplanted with spring bulbs such as hyacinths, followed by petunias. Even within such an elementary scheme there is scope for numerous color variations.

The undiluted color of massed bedding plants – the vibrant red, for example, of *Salvia splendens* – is not to everyone's taste. But it is perfectly possible to create subtle color schemes, using short-lived plants such as some of the hardy annuals. These can be sown in the open ground to form drifts that merge into one another. The blues of cornflower and nigella, for example, go well with the soft pinks of clarkia or the mixed colors of larkspur and shirley poppies. It is worth experimenting with these short-term color effects, the most successful of which could be translated into long-term schemes using herbaceous perennials.

Where herbaceous perennials have already been planted but have not yet reached maturity, you can put in short-term planting that in color will complement (or, if you prefer, contrast with) the long-term scheme. For example, in a traditional border where the gray-leaved perennials include *Artemisia ludoviciana* and *Festuca glauca*, gaps can be filled with the annual *Senecio maritima* and taller *Centaurea gymnocarpa*, both with gray-toned foliage. A border all in whites and creams can look stunning: with the white-flowered *Anemone × hybrida* 'Honorine Jobert' and *Chrysanthemum maximum* you could combine white sweet peas, baby's breath and petunias. In shades of pink, a core of pink penstemons, malva, monarda, phlox and sedums could be supplemented with pink sweet peas, cosmos, pelargoniums, stocks

Left: Vegetables, combined with ornamentals, offer a wealth of unexpected textures, making a splendid central feature. This would be an appealing option for a small garden. A formal layout, with some good permanent planting, will sustain interest even though some of the plants are short-lived. Here, foliage and flowers of herbs and vegetables are set against more permanent features, including standard roses, box edging, a small box centerpiece and a bold design of attractively patterned narrow paths.

Below: Reserve plants that can be dropped into borders to fill gaps will help to keep the garden colorful over a long season. Lilies, seen here with a tobacco plant, make spectacular star performers, many being richly scented, as well as sumptuous in form and color. The tobacco plant (*Nicotiana alata*) is a deliciously fragrant half-hardy annual, flowering (white) in late summer.

and impatiens. To the mauve and purple *Salvia turkestanica, S. haematodes* and delphiniums you could add mauve sweet peas, petunias heliotrope and verbena. For a hot color composition in strong yellows, oranges and russets, the yellow and bronze *Anthemis* 'E.C. Buxton', *Achillea filipendulina* 'Gold Plate', *Crocosmia* 'Lucifer' and *Sedum* 'Atropurpureum' would look well with a short-term planting of rudbeckia, pot marigold, tagetes and zinnias. And finally with the red *Lobelia cardinalis, Dahlia* 'Bishop of Llandaff' and *Iresine* you could plant red verbena, begonias, pinky prince's feather (*Amaranthus hypochondriacus*) and red (or white) nicotiana. Many variations can be played on these themes, and the interest of the borders extended by a planting of spring bulbs such as daffodils and tulips, perhaps combined with wallflowers, pansies or forget-me-not.

Even when herbaceous or mixed borders are mature, it is useful to have a few short-term plants growing in pots that can be dropped in to fill gaps. There is a good precedent for this method of "cheating", as it was favored by Gertrude Jekyll, perhaps the most influential gardener of the late Victorian and Edwardian period. She always kept a few pots of hydrangeas ready to pop in to a gap or bring color to the border in the late summer. She was gardening on a scale that few, if any, would now attempt, and maintaining a reserve was not a problem. In a small garden, however, space is at a premium and you may not be able to run to the luxury of a "pot park".

There is probably no finer example of vegetables used ornamentally than the famous French garden of Villandry. Much of the formal layout in the 17th-century manner consists of parterres planted with vegetables, where the best use is made of interesting color and form. There are many attractive vegetables suitable for a *potager* of a more domestic scale. Among the most colorful and decorative are salad crops such as lettuces (romaine, red and green oak-leaved and butter-head) and radishes, different kinds of cabbages, including ornamental varieties, beans of all sorts (climbing varieties can be trained up twig teepees), patty pans and gourds, zucchini, Swiss and ruby chard, celery, leeks, carrots, tomatoes, brussels sprouts and beet. To these can be added perennials such as artichokes and sorrel, chives, parsley and other herbs, small fruits such as strawberries, and a few flowers – pansies, daisies, forget-me-not and the like – for color. Picking vegetables may spoil the visual effect, but then you have the pleasure of eating them. At a practical level I have found that devoting the garden to vegetables during its first few years is the most satisfying way of using the ground while becoming familiar with its potential.

Below, right: **It is especially in late summer that it is useful to have fillers for flower borders. Here 'Marmalade', a cultivar of the annual rudbeckia, and** *Nicotiana alata* **'Domino Lime' help to bulk out a border that includes perennial sedums and asters.**

THE POTTED GARDEN

Growing plants in pots is as old as gardening itself, and its popularity all around the world is shown in countless balcony gardens, informal arrangements on terraces and in courtyards, and grand formal designs. In any garden, whatever its size or age, pot-grown plants are invaluable components, allowing great flexibility in the staging of effects. Suitable plants of infinite variety can be moved around to suit mood and season. Well-chosen groups can make harmonious compositions, or pots can be strategically placed to create or else to underline a formal arrangement. Moreover, plants that need winter protection can be taken out in the summer months as oranges and lemons were in the great gardens of the 17th and 18th centuries. Yet another advantage of gardening in pots is that it allows you to grow plants that would not be suitable for the soil conditions in your garden. Camellias and rhododendrons, for example, are lime-hating, so that if you live in an alkaline area it will not be possible to grow them satisfactorily in the open ground. But even in such areas they can be grown in large tubs of peaty soil, if they are irrigated with rain water and not tap water, which is likely to be alkaline.

Almost any plant can be grown in a container, if it is given the necessary care, but it may not grow as big or live as long as it would in the open ground. Some plants, of course, are better suited to growing in pots than others. These tend to come from drier parts of the world, such as the Mediterranean region. Tolerance of dry conditions is, however, not the only relevant factor. For example, some plants are unhappy if their roots are restricted. Even forest trees such as beech, hornbeam and pines can be pot-grown; but, although not pruned and trained rigorously in the Japanese manner, they will tend to take on the appearance of bonsai.

Woody plants, especially evergreens, are particularly useful for sustaining interest throughout the year and giving the garden a distinctive character. Box and yew are familiar evergreens, but others that were favored in the 17th and 18th century deserve to be more widely used now. These include *Rhamnus alaternus angustifolia*, *Phillyrea angustifolia*, *Viburnum tinus* and *Pyracantha coccinea*. The striking shapes of clipped specimens make positive statements in the garden. Although deciduous trees and shrubs make their greatest contribution from spring to autumn, many look beautiful even without leaves. Among hardy deciduous species that do well in pots are *Viburnum opulus*, *Hamamelis mollis* and the Japanese maples, including the many small forms of *Acer palmatum* and *A. japonicum*. There are compact, less vigorous cultivars of many species – for example, *Viburnum opulus* 'Compactum' is a form of the guelder rose that has a particularly neat habit – and these are better suited to pot culture than the species.

Many gardeners concentrate on summer planting at the expense of the other seasons, but there are bulbs, annuals and perennials that will extend the period of enjoyment. The following are plants that I look out for with special pleasure, but the range is vast and there is plenty of scope for making a personal selection. I could never go through a spring without at least a few daffodils – the early-flowering 'February Gold', for example, or the pure white 'Thalia'. There are larger and more showy forms that I like, too, such as 'Orangerie' and 'Gigantic Star'. Daffodils can be planted in tiers and when combined with other bulbs such as bright-blue grape hyacinths (*Muscari armeniacum*) will make a beautiful display. A pot of sweet-smelling hyacinths is always a pleasure to have, and you can choose from pink, yellow, blue or white varieties. Later, at tulip time, the creamy white *T. fosteriana* 'Purissima' is delightful with blue forget-me-not.

There are so many possibilities in the summer that one is spoilt for choice. Pelargoniums, in clear white or brilliant red, are probably my favorites. They can be grown alone or with alyssum and lobelia. Alternatively, pink *Verbena* 'Sissinghurst' and the trailing gray *Helichrysum petiolare* would make an arresting combination. Other candidates, on their own or in mixes, include begonias, coleus, marguerites, nasturtiums, osteospermum, nemesias or petunias. Among good foliage plants, I particularly like the golden-leaved *Ballota* and the silver-leaved *Senecio maritima*.

Dwarf asters and chrysanthemums would cheer you up through the autumn, and steadfast plants for winter include trailing variegated ivies and dwarf conifers. Tiny *Iris reticulata* or *I. danfordiae* herald the end of the cold season and a pot of pansies can also be comforting seen through a window in late winter.

The choice of the pot or container is itself important. Plastic pots have some practical advantages over those made of clay. The evaporation through the walls of clay pots dries and cools the potting compost, whereas in plastic containers the roots remain warmer and moister. However, the red clay pot is a beautiful thing in itself and weathers extremely well. Not all clay pots, or even glazed ones, are frost-proof and, if they are not, they must be brought inside in winter. Stone troughs and urns make bold statements in a design but they are expensive and difficult to obtain. Fortunately, some substitutes cast in composite stone or concrete are of reasonable quality. Wood can also be very effective, particularly when used to construct Versailles planters, which can be built to any size. The

Bulbs are among the showiest of plants for late winter and spring, and most are excellent subjects for containers. The shorter-growing tulips, such as *Tulipa greigii*, shown here with winter-flowering pansies, stand up well to wind and provide a cheerful sight when the days are still chilly. Flowering in mid- to late spring, *T. greigii* hybrids have the additional interest of striped or mottled leaves, often with wavy edges. Examples include 'Red Riding Hood', whose leaves are striped purple and green; and 'Dreamboat', whose amber-yellow flowers tinged with red are offset by brown-striped gray-green foliage.

larger ones are easier to handle if they are on wheels and if the sides can be removed to allow the soil to be renewed.

No special skills are needed to grow plants in containers successfully. The aim is to keep plants healthy but not so vigorous that they outgrow their pots within a season. It is important to use a good-quality potting compost, either soil- or peat-based, and the addition of a few pieces of charcoal will help to keep it sweet. If you are preparing your own compost, mix in a slow-release fertilizer to ensure that plants get all the nutrients they need. In the case of plants kept in the same container for more than one year, work a little slow-release fertilizer into the compost at the beginning of each growing season. Some plants in large pots can be left in the same container for many years, provided that the top 4 to 6 inches (10-15cm) of compost are renewed annually at the beginning of the growing season; when scraping away the old compost, take care not to damage the roots of the plant. Most plants, however, need to be moved on to larger pots with new compost and fertilizer after one or two years. In general, plants benefit from additional feeding with a liquid foliar or soil fertilizer during the height of the growing season. Continue feeding annuals right to the end of summer, but with trees and shrubs ease off after mid-summer so that the wood has time to ripen before winter.

Watering plants in pots is the major task and it must be done regularly throughout the growing season. During a dry spell this may mean daily or even twice daily. The amount of water required by plants is almost always underestimated. Standing pots in trays helps watering during dry spells. In showery weather the trays serve as reservoirs, but they must be emptied when there are longer periods of rain, or the compost will become waterlogged.

Far left: Traditional stone troughs, which are suitable for low-growing plants, including alpines, make impressive features. They are difficult to obtain, and expensive, but as a money-saving alternative you could buy an attractive imitation stone trough which will age to blend with other features of the garden. These troughs (shown in early summer) have been arranged on a paved area next to steps to provide extra space for low-growing perennials and bring them nearer to eye level. Brick-built containers provide an additional level of interest. The terraced effect is very successful, showing the advantage of grouping containers that differ in their depth.

This page, top: Lightweight containers can be arranged in groups that are changed according to what plants are in season. Here, a cast-iron ornament provides a focus for a spring composition of Narcissus 'Cheerfulness', polyanthus, primulas and an azalea, in terracotta pots.

This page, bottom left: The shape, texture and color of a container can sometimes count for as much as the ornamental quality of the plants grown in it. This old weathered urn punctuating a stone wall contains a simple planting of spring-flowering auriculas.

Near left: Versailles planters of white-painted wood are versatile containers for formal gardens. Here, a yellow and white arrangement of tender plants – white petunias, Chrysanthemum frutescens, yellow-flowered Bidens ferulaefolia and round-leaved Helichrysum petiolare 'Limelight' – makes a cool combination.

INSTANT CAMOUFLAGE

The essence of camouflage is restraint, otherwise undue attention is drawn to the very thing that should be hidden. With successful camouflaging, whatever is offensive to the eye merges into the background. Skilful planting is often the best way to mask an eyesore outside the garden boundaries or to camouflage an unattractive feature within the garden. Fast-growing trees can be used to hide an obtrusive building, and there are many climbers and wall plants that can transform an ugly wall or shed, either as a temporary solution or more permanently. There are, however, other ways of dealing with the unsightly, combined if you wish with planting, that will give an almost instant effect.

With walls, sheds and other buildings within a garden a coat of paint can go a long way to making them easier on the eye. In temperate lighting conditions, choose a neutral color such as gray, soft green, soft blue, or white broken with pink or brown. Crisp white and bright greens, blues and yellows are more appropriate where sunlight is stronger.

In a small garden with a large flat wall there is scope for creating an ambitious painted *trompe l'œil* scene, a giant perspective of architecture or garden. To transform the garden it needs to be treated with conviction, and it will help to integrate the scene with the whole if the edges are blurred by planting. The technique has an ancient pedigree and was particularly used in Roman times, when the walls surrounding a courtyard were commonly decorated with birds, animals and plants, garden scenes with fountains and pools, and even views of lakes and mountains.

Trellis is a particularly useful material for camouflaging and masking, and always looks at home in the garden. If it is to be painted, the color must be chosen with care. It is often better to use a different tone of the color against which it is going to be set, rather than a contrasting color. Trellis can be fashioned into an intricate *trompe l'œil* after the 18th-century French manner or it can be a simple pattern of diamonds or squares. Fix the panels discreetly but securely, and use the trellis as an opportunity to grow climbers that need support.

Fast-growing climbers include the perennial Russian vine (*Polygonum aubertii*), the glory vine (*Vitis coignetiae*) and oriental bittersweet (*Celastrus orbiculatus*). These are vigorous enough to grow 10 feet (3m) in a year and are especially useful in difficult shady spots where little else will grow but where their vigor will be checked. Less vigorous but equally rewarding each year is the perennial pea (*Lathyrus latifolius*), which usually has mauvy pink flowers but is stunning in its white form. It dies down in the winter but reaches up to 6 to 7 feet (2m) in summer. *Clematis montana* and its forms such as 'Rubens' and 'Elizabeth' will also quickly cover a shed, in spring, flowering in cascades of white or pale pink that spread a delightful scent said to resemble vanilla – I think it just smells of itself.

If it is difficult to attach any sort of support to a wall, then self-clingers are the answer. The hardiest of all is perhaps Boston ivy (*Parthenocissus tricuspidata* 'Veitchii'), which has bright crimson leaves in the autumn. The English ivy (*Hedera helix*), of course, will also attach itself to any surface it encounters and gives an otherwise uninteresting garage or shed a romantic air. It becomes established quickly and then makes steady growth. Look out for one of its many interesting cultivars, some of

Opposite page: In one season the golden hop (*Humulus lupulus* 'Aureus') will grow to more than 15 feet (4.6m), given ideal conditions. A herbaceous perennial, it will die right back to the crown in winter. The coloring is best if the plant receives full sunlight, although the roots prefer shade.
Far left, this page: Against a warm sunny wall *Clematis armandii* will flower well in spring. Just beside the window is a young plant of *Lavatera* 'Barnsley'.
Near left: The same scene in summer a year later. The clematis has reached the top of the wall and the *Lavatera* almost completely obscures the Gothic window.

which are hardier than others. 'Triloba', 'Digitata' and 'Hibernica' are particularly quick-growing and have wide or very dissected leaves; the latter has in addition a variegated form with the most attractive creamy-yellow markings. There are some smaller-leaved, slightly less vigorous selections that are more suited to a small building. A good example is the bright green 'Angularis', which also has a variegated form. If left to grow unchecked and into the light, ivies develop mature forms in which the leaves lose their lobed shape and become more elliptical. In the late summer, bees are attracted to umbels of yellow flowers and black berries follow.

Not all ugly walls and sheds are in the shade. In a sheltered sunny spot where you can provide extra winter protection in the early years and plenty of moisture throughout the summer, the trumpet vine, *Campsis radicans*, will make a great show with its bright orange or red trumpet-like flowers. Once established it is quite hardy, provided that the wood has ripened sufficiently. Potash applied around the roots in the autumn will help harden the wood. While, strictly speaking, climbers such as the trumpet vine do not offer "instant" solutions, combined with other measures they can very quickly transform a somewhat dreary prospects.

SEASON BY SEASON

Changing effects through the seasons are one of the greatest pleasures the garden offers, even in a plot that is predominantly clothed in evergreens. From the emergence of spring bulbs to the more austere delights of winter, the unfolding year presents a shifting pattern of pleasures – that is, provided that the garden has been well planned and cultivated.

The following section of the book looks at the ways in which seasonal change can be exploited for maximum benefit – whether by creating an all-year garden, or by contriving spectacular effects in one particular season. Due emphasis is placed on the composition of carefully coordinated flower effects, but with plenty of detail too on the delights offered by foliage, fruit, berries and bark.

A special feature of this section is the inclusion of specific planting "programs" for three particular borders timed to give their best in spring, summer and autumn, with suggestions for extending the season, and for creating short-term interest in the first year.

CREATING ALL-YEAR INTEREST

When visiting gardens I am often told, "You should have seen it last week," or "If you want to see anything of interest, you should come in the spring – it's just a symphony in green in the summer." But despite missing what owners see as the highlights of their garden calendar, I commonly find plenty of interest to look at. Invariably the gardens that hold their own through all seasons of the year show two characteristics. The first is a matter of design – a strong framework of hedges, walls and paths that gives interesting vistas and an element of surprise. The second is a matter of imaginative planting – a wide range of material used to make the most of foliage, fruit, bark, form and habit as well as floral display throughout the whole year.

The vagaries of the weather make it impossible to predict on exactly which day a plant will "perform" and, indeed, how long it will be at its peak. However, the broad lines of the succession remain fairly constant, so an effective planting plan can easily be drawn up to provide something to admire – or, at least, to anticipate admiring – on most days of the year.

In late spring, herbaceous perennials slowly take over from and cover the space left by the bulbs as they fade and die down; shrubs flower in succession and come into fruit; climbers cover pergolas and walls and some, such as roses, clematis and flame nasturtium (*Tropaeolum speciosum*), can be persuaded to grow through shrubs and trees to flower before or after these. Inevitably there is an occasional lull when there are vacant spaces, such as the hiatus between the spring and summer annual

A great wrought-iron basket planted with yucca and golden variegated euonymus is the focal point in the middle of a pool. In early spring (far right, top) the basket appears to stand high above the water on its pedestal, but as the months progress it becomes part of the planting around it. Only daffodils (to the left of the feature) and the emerging leaves of day lilies (*Hemerocallis*) and variegated iris make a show in the damp water margin. By the early summer (far right, below) the day lilies together with some pink, white and mauve aquilegias are in flower. By now the astilbe foliage has fully unfolded. In late summer (large picture) the pale astilbes are in flower. Throughout the year the main emphasis of the color scheme is yellow and cream.

Page 90: In a well-designed garden there are good foliage and flowering plants for every season. Spring is the season for moisture-loving plants that like cool conditions. Here, in a damp sunny corner, the magenta flowers of *Primula pulverulenta* are complemented by the pale pink aquilegia. The accent provided by the variegated sword-like leaves of *Iris pseudacorus* 'Variegata' gives form and strength to the compositon.

Right: A dramatic treatment of hard surfaces can help to support plant interest through the year. Here, the turning space for a car has been laid in granite blocks and gravel around a commemorative plaque, bringing to mind the pattern of an ancient monastic turf maze. Bordered by an evergreen yucca which contrasts strikingly with a tall *Cedrus atlantica* 'Glauca' and two squat golden yews, this feature serves as a kind of amphitheater from which the plants can be appreciated.

Far right: This secluded corner in a pinetum has been designed to look good whatever the season. The path of granite blocks curves gently around a bed of conifers in which cobbles have been used as ground cover, lending a Japanese air to the scene. The stone seating is framed by a trained weeping Atlantic cedar, which makes an unusual arbor. Notice how the different sizes and shapes of stones make an interesting composition within a particular color range – just as the evergreen foliage does.

plantings. But when beds of pansies or other spring-flowering plants are cleared to make way for plantings of nicotiana or pelargoniums, growth is quick and the space is soon filled.

Drawing up a planting plan for year-round interest is essential if you are to achieve some of the most exciting effects of which your garden is capable. Interesting color sequences and coincidences of coordinated tones (see Color Composition, pp.104-15), are the hallmarks of accomplished gardening, and need careful planning. Even if you are primarily concerned with achieving a succession of well-matched flowers, the value of foliage should not be underestimated. It provides a background and foil for color schemes but itself changes endlessly, offering great scope for use on its own and to fill gaps in the floral calendar (see also Foliage and Framework, pp.116-18).

Some plants are of outstanding value in the all-season garden, either because they have a very long season of interest, perhaps flowering for months on end, or because they have more than one season of interest. It may be that they have attractive flowers in spring followed by colorful fruit in late summer, and there may even be the bonus of variegated or colored foliage for much of the year or attractive bark in the winter. These plants are discussed more fully in the chapter on Special Performers (pp. 98-103) but one example will give an idea of their value. *Viburnum opulus* 'Aureum' is outstanding for its clusters of white flowers in spring, which are followed by heavy crops of showy red berries in autumn, and the whole time the plant is in leaf it is a mass of bright golden foliage.

The particular character of each season should not be neglected in the search for ways of making a year-round garden. The

Six points of a yew hedge serve as an evergreen landmark in this unusual garden. In early spring (far right, below) hellebores and daffodils are in flower, while peonies, delphiniums and irises are appearing through a patchy covering of snow. In early summer (large picture, right) aquilegias and astrantias are in bloom, while the sun highlights the young pink growth of *Pieris*. After the peonies and delphiniums (not shown in flower in this sequence) comes the turn of the phlox in pinks and mauve (below). Note how the hedges have a fuzzy outline in this picture: they are shortly to be trimmed. By the autumn (far right, top) the lines are clean, ready to carry the garden through the winter. The dead flower heads are due for cutting down. In the foreground *Nerine bowdenii* stands out against the glaucous foliage: its pink flowers are borne on 2-feet (60cm) stems.

seasons should be emphasized by a sequence of highlights created by a succession of plants, even though their dazzling performance or subtle beauty may be short-lived.

Some plants, such as *Anemone nemorosa*, disappear discreetly, giving way to larger and later foliage plants that cover the ground they occupy. More problematic are those that after flowering go through a period of being more or less untidy, such as daffodils and oriental poppies, or nondescript, such as a number of shrubs, including forsythia, lilacs, spiraea, buddleia, philadelphus and laburnum. They are all beautiful in flower, mark the seasons and are wonderfully effective in providing focal points; but then they present a problem. The unsightly foliage of some perennials can be masked by the growth of others that follow on; baby's breath, for example, if planted in front of oriental poppies, will cover their untidy leaves. Pruning shrubs after flowering removes unsightly dead flowers and uninteresting seed pods. In the case of robust shrubs, it may be worth using them as frames for climbers such as a clematis, for then there will be at least two seasons of flower.

In a large garden there is also scope for devoting whole areas to a single season. In her famous garden at Sissinghurst Castle in Kent, Vita Sackville-West, the celebrated English garden writer, created the nut walk, which was underplanted with polyanthus to give a spectacular spring display. But in summer and autumn the white and red gardens were her main focus of interest. In many small gardens it would not be sensible to condemn one area to mark time for most of the year. A much better course is to emphasize a seasonal theme in a border while ensuring that the border is also sufficiently well furnished with plants that will be attractive at other times of the year.

SPECIAL PERFORMERS

In any garden, but particularly a small garden, plants that give a long display, repeat a performance or stage more than one act, are especially valuable. Many of the best garden plants gain points on several counts. They may have beautiful flowers followed by attractive seed pods or fruit; the foliage may be as important or more important than the flowers on account of its texture, shape or color; the plant may have an interesting architectural form that enhances the beauty of flowers and leaves; and there may be richly colored bark or twigs that can become points of interest in the winter garden. There will always be a place for plants that make a dazzling brief performance. However, a garden that relies on these exclusively risks being dull over long periods of the year: lasting performers are needed to sustain the garden through all four seasons.

Plants with long flowering seasons are among the most useful, yet the way in which they can sustain the garden's interest is overlooked by many gardeners. Most plants that start to bloom in the early part of the year tend to have short seasons, whereas from late spring right through to the end of the summer it is possible to find species that flower continuously for two, three or sometimes four months. There are also some plants that will flower twice during the year, provided that they have been carefully deadheaded after the first blooming.

Although it is true that, on the whole, trees and shrubs have shorter flowering seasons than perennials and annuals, there are some remarkable exceptions. *Prunus × subhirtella* 'Autumnalis' begins to bloom in late autumn or early winter and is spangled with small, palest pink flowers right through until early spring; as a bonus it has attractive autumn foliage. Two viburnums that also have pale pink flowers, the deciduous *V. farreri* and the evergreen *V. tinus*, carry clusters of these throughout most of the winter. The latter often has the previous season's crop of blue-black berries at the same time, and *V. farreri* has richly scented flowers.

From late spring until early autumn *Potentilla fruticosa*, a shrub that does best in full sun but will tolerate some shade, displays a long succession of yellow or orange flowers. Over much the same period the evergreen, slightly tender Mexican orange (*Choisya ternata*) bears scented white flowers that stand out well against the glossy aromatic foliage.

Some of the roses are among the most valuable long-flowering plants, the modern hybrid teas and floribundas blooming almost continuously throughout the summer. The new classification, by which these are known respectively as large-flowered and cluster-flowered bush roses, has not yet displaced the more familiar names. Since 'La France', the first hybrid tea, was introduced in 1867, many hundreds of varieties have been raised, and of these probably none has achieved greater fame than 'Peace'. My own favourites among the most hardy include the orange-red 'Dolly Parton', salmon-pink 'Michèle Meilland' and amber-yellow 'Whisky Mac'. Many of the floribundas make good bedding roses, and outstanding varieties include the bright yellow 'Allgold', deep crimson 'Europeana' and the white 'Iceberg'. The vigorous pink-flowered 'Queen Elizabeth' is one of the best in this category, but unfortunately it is too tall and upright to be well suited to bedding schemes.

The hybrid teas and floribundas are not the only roses that are repeat-flowering. There are numerous old and modern varieties, described as recurrent, remontant and, in some cases less accurately, perpetual, that flower over a long season or produce more than one flush of blooms in a year. My own favorites include apricot-yellow 'Buff Beauty', 'Cécile Brunner', whose tiny pink flowers are exquisite in bud, crimson 'Cerise Bouquet', richly scented 'Madame Isaac Pereire' with crimson flowers, white 'Nevada', purple 'Reine des Violettes' and pale pink 'Stanwell Perpetual'. Most of the rambler roses flower only once, although both 'Aimée Vibert' and 'Albéric Barbier' have extended seasons. Among the modern climbers there are a number that repeat reliably, including exceptionally vigorous varieties such as the single-flowered yellow 'Mermaid', and relatively short-growing pillar roses such as the pink 'Aloha'. Among older varieties I like the pink bourbon 'Kathleen Harrop'.

Bedding plants such as lobelia, pelargoniums and petunias are well known for their long flowering season, but there are also many perennials that give a long display, and a carefully chosen selection will give nearly non-stop flowering throughout the summer. In the early part of the season, geraniums such as *G. endressii*, *G.* 'Claridge Druce' and *G. wallichianum* 'Buxton Variety' will put on a show of pink and blue flowers. *Campanula portenschlagiana* has a profusion of blue flowers throughout the summer and is tolerant of the most inhospitable sites; beware, though, for it is invasive and will swamp choice plants. The shrubby rock and sun roses (*Helianthemum nummularium*) and *Cistus* × *crispus* 'Sunset' bloom for about two months, while *Salvia superba* 'May Night' lasts for nearly four. Lasting perennials that flower from midsummer on include *Penstemon barbatus*,

A group of plants that has been providing interest and color throughout the summer is still looking good in early autumn. The gray-blue foliage of festuca and *Alchemilla mollis* contrasts with the yellow flowers of potentilla. The golden foliage of the false acacia (*Robina pseudoacacia* 'Frisia') is highlighted by the purple sedum.

Lavatera 'Barnsley' flowers continuously for almost the whole summer. It is easily grown from cuttings taken in late summer and overwintered in a frost-free spot. It will grow 4 feet (1.2m) or more in the first season.

Diascia rigescens, fuchsias, *Lavatera*, followed by *Phlox paniculata, Aster × frikartii* 'Mönch, rudbeckias, hydrangeas and the often neglected *Cimicifuga* species.

Polygonum bistorta 'Superbum' not only has a long flowering season but also has foliage that gradually turns a glowing red in autumn. It is one of a number of good perennials that make a major contribution to the garden on two fronts. On a modest scale, good flowering plants such as peonies, dicentras and the evergreen hellebores have delightful foliage which provides a gentle background to other border plants. On an altogether grander scale, *Acanthus spinosus* has handsome dull-green spiny leaves and spikes of purplish flowers that can reach 5 feet (1.5m). As a good contrast you could plant bergenias that flower in early spring and have huge leathery round leaves that cover the ground; or *Rosa glauca*, a rose with blue-gray leaves and bluish-pink single flowers that coincide with the flowering of the acanthus.

A number of herbaceous plants with interesting flowers also have good silver or gray foliage. The stately *Onopordum acanthium* has thistle-like gray foliage and purple flowers, while *Eryngium giganteum* has similar attributes but is less than half its height, reaching 3 feet (1.5m). Both are biennials and sow themselves freely, thriving in dry sunny situations. Also with gray leaves and enjoying similar conditions are the little *Convolvulus cneorum*, which carries a long succession of pink and white flowers, and the tall Californian poppy (*Romneya coulteri*), which has splendid white flowers. These are both perennials but are on the tender side, and even in reasonably mild areas it is worth overwintering cuttings in case specimens outdoors are lost.

There are also shrubs and trees that combine pleasing gray foliage with other features. *Pyrus salicifolia* 'Pendula' and *Hippophae rhamnoides* have fine silvery foliage and attractive fruit – small pears (inedible) on the pyrus and bright orange berries on the sea buckthorn.

Not many purple-leaved plants also have attractive flowers, but this makes the few there are all the more precious. Among the perennials *Heuchera* 'Palace Purple' makes a bold splash of deep-colored rounded foliage with white flowers in early summer. *Lobelia fulgens* and *L. cardinalis* hybrids have tall spikes of red flowers above beet-red foliage. Of woody plants, *Cotinus coggygria* 'Notcutt's Variety', the purple smoke tree, has a rounded habit to 8 feet (2.5m) with a haze of purple flowers in summer. *Weigela florida* 'Foliis Purpurea' is a dwarf form with purple-flushed leaves and pink flowers.

Another form of *W. florida*, 'Variegata', has beautiful variegated leaves and pink flowers. Together with *Cornus controversa* 'Variegata', which has great tiers of white bracted flowers in the early summer, and *Daphne odora* 'Aureo-marginata', which has fragrant pink flowers in the early spring, this ranks among the most gardenworthy of variegated shrubs.

There are many perennials with variegated leaves that look good when the plants have finished flowering. Among my favorites are the evergreen *Brunnera macrophylla* 'Dawson's White', which has blue flowers in the spring, and the herbaceous *Phlox paniculata* 'Norah Leigh'. *Arum italicum* 'Pictum' has leaves that are mottled with gray and creamy variegations in spring and spikes of red fruit in the autumn.

Good autumn leaf color is a bonus with many deciduous trees and shrubs that have already made a good floral display. The winter-flowering *Corylopsis pauciflora* and *Hamamelis mollis* and spring-flowering *Cercis canadensis* and *Rhododendron luteum* all turn to shades of yellow and orange in the autumn, as do the roses *R. virginiana* and *R. setigera*, which both additionally have attractive stems to see them through the winter. It is often forgotten that there are perennials with good autumn foliage. *Epimedium* species and *Geranium macrorrhizum* are two flowering ground-cover plants that have attractive autumn tints.

Young spring foliage can be quite as pleasing as the showy displays of autumn. The shoots and leaves of peonies, for example, are beautifully colored as they come up through the ground. Among the most spectacular of spring leaves is the young growth of *Pieris* species and hybrids. The shrubs in this acid-loving genus have beautiful young coppery or brilliant red foliage in late winter. In spring there are long panicles of tiny bell-shaped, slightly scented flowers.

Fruit can be a great attraction in the autumn, and there are many species that produce abundant crops. In some cases birds very quickly move in for the attack, but on some plants the fruits are likely to escape unscathed.

The red hips of *Rosa glauca* have a very short season, but the orange ones of *R. moyesii*, its cultivar 'Geranium' and *R. macrophylla* last well. *Rosa rugosa* and its cultivars have large fleshy vermilion hips that are flat in shape and last until they rot; the fruit is preceded by double or single flowers in white and shades of pink, and the foliage turns golden yellow after the hips have formed.

Other shrubs that produce a plentiful crop of fruit in the autumn include the cotoneasters, which flower in late spring. The gaunt pyracantha, which can be covered in flowers in summer, followed by a plentiful and lasting display of fruit, tolerates shade and does well against a wall or alternatively serves as an impenetrable hedge. Black berries are a striking feature in autumn of the Oregon grape (*Mahonia aquifolium*); in the spring rich yellow flowers grace this architectural plant, which grows in most situations, whether in sun or in shade. Viburnums, dogwoods, chaenomeles, skimmia and amelanchier also deserve mention among the good garden shrubs that have beautiful flowers in spring or summer and an autumn display of fruit.

Moving on to trees, several genera are outstanding for the way their attractive flowers are followed by handsome fruit. Many of the *Sorbus* have white or pale pink flowers and showy fruit in autumn. The fruits of the mountain ash or rowan (*S. aucuparia*) are red, orange or yellow, but are too palatable to birds to last long; however, the white fruits of *S. cashmiriana* endure well into the winter. The various crab apples (*Malus*) have white or pink flowers followed by red fruit, as in the cultivars 'John Downie', 'Red Jade' and 'Red Sentinel', or yellow fruit, as in 'Golden Hornet'. The hawthorns (*Crataegus*) generally carry white blossom in great abundance and in autumn bear red fruit that coincides with good autumn tints.

Climbers too can earn their keep by performing twice in the year. The humble honeysuckle (*Lonicera periclymenum*) has sweetly scented beautiful flowers that in late summer are followed by translucent berries. The yellow flowers of *Clematis tangutica* start in mid-summer, and the first silky seed heads overlap with the last blooms. *Akebia quinata* has fragrant racemes of dark red to purple flowers from mid-spring onward, and after a hot summer produces dark purple, sausage-shaped fruits, which split to reveal black seeds and white pulpy flesh. The passionflower (*Pas-siflora caerulea*) is another climber that produces fruit, in this case orange and egg-shaped, after a favorable summer However, the plant's main attraction is the extraordinary tiered flowers that are borne in early summer.

Perennials and bulbous plants that have attractive seed heads are few but valuable, as they last well into the winter when, covered in frost, they add a special quality to the garden. *Sedum* 'Autumn Joy' has pale green flower heads in bud for much of the summer, opening to pink in the autumn, and flat seed heads that can be left until spring before being cut down. Peonies can be allowed to drop their petals and form large seed pods, which open to reveal shiny black seeds. *Crambe cordifolia*, *Angelica archangelica* and *Heracleum mantegazzianum* bear huge panicles of seed heads which, if allowed to go their own way, will produce quantities of seedlings. Long seed pods follow the red or yellow summer flowers of the horned poppy (*Glaucium flavum*), while round flat ones follow the white or purple spring flowers of honesty (*Lunaria annua*). *Iris foetidissima* flowers in summer and has bright orange seed in split pods from the autumn until the beginning of spring.

A feature of the winter garden, as beautiful in its way as the more obvious delights of summer, is the bark of certain trees, many of which are valuable also for their flowers and foliage. Like so many winter flowers that have a quiet beauty, the barks of specimen trees are best appreciated at close quarters, especially when lit by a low winter sun. Among the loveliest are the highly polished dark brown barks of some of the flowering cherry hybrids and the pale flaking bark (corky when young) of the Turkish hazel (*Corylus colurna*), a tree that in spring is covered with yellow catkins. Maples are famous for their bark as well as their autumn color, two of the most striking being *Acer griseum*, with papery cinnamon-colored bark, and *A. palmatum* 'Sango-kaku', with bright red branches.

For a bigger impact there are a few shrubs that, if cut hard back in the spring, throw up brightly colored stems. Perhaps the most famous and commonly encountered is *Cornus alba*. The best form of this for winter color is without doubt 'Sibirica', but the cultivars 'Elegantissima' and 'Spaethii' have good variegated foliage for the summer months. *Rubus cockburnianus*, a relative of the raspberry, has dark stems covered in a silvery bloom that shows up well, as do its white-backed leaves, in the summer, against a dark evergreen hedge. Willows, particularly *Salix alba* 'Vitellina,' with bright orange-yellow stems, and *S. daphnoides*, with purple stems, both bear catkins in spring, white in *S. alba* and tinged with purple in *S. daphnoides*.

The plants I have described here, which either have a long flowering season or put on more than one show across the seasons, are thoroughbreds, and obviously deserve their place in any garden. For my part, I sometimes think that I could live without the sprinters and dazzlers, certain that my ideal garden of lasting and repeat performers would give ample pleasure throughout the year.

Left: *Euphorbia characias wulfenii*, an evergreen sub-shrub, is one of the best all-year performers. It flowers for two months in late spring and has a stately presence for the rest of the year, thanks to its blue-green foliage. The plant looks its best when treated as an isolated specimen, rather than in groups.

Pyracantha 'Orange Glow' is a mass of small white flowers in early summer (below). In the autumn these give way to bright orange berries (bottom). This easy-to-grow evergreen will perform well even in difficult sites. It should be pruned in late summer.

COLOR COMPOSITION

Few things in gardening are as rewarding as the execution of a successful color scheme that evolves over a period of time. However, it has to be admitted that this takes some experience, and that the process of learning is likely to be punctuated with errors. It makes sense, therefore, to start on a modest scale, experimenting in small areas – perhaps at the same time as concentrating on developing the framework of a new garden. Working with annuals and biennials is easiest, as with these short-lived plants any mistakes can be rectified quickly. With longer-lived plants it is useful to work with just two or three kinds that can be moved without difficulty if the effect turns out to be disappointing. Your initial scheme might consist of no more than a combination of two foliage plants, one with large and one with small leaves, and a single flowering plant for color. Other plants can be added to this core as more experience is gained.

The main color themes of the gardening year can be organized into a simplified "color calendar", which the gardener should bear in mind when planning effects through the seasons. There are many exceptions to the pattern I describe below: however, it does offer a basic framework on which to build.

Many early spring plants are pale yellow and blue. The earliest shrubs include the yellow-flowered *Cornus mas, Corylopsis pauciflora*, and one of the loveliest of the witch hazels, *Hamamelis mollis* 'Pallida'; for underplanting in yellow there are daffodils, primroses and a showy, bushy euphorbia, *E. polychroma*. Among the blues are the little *Iris histrioides* 'Major', *Omphalodes verna* and blue hyacinths. In spring there are pink flowers, too, at first pale but

becoming more vivid as the season progresses. Care must be taken not to mix the yellows and the pinks, because they clash unforgivably, as do other color combinations later in the year. A forsythia, such as 'Spring Glory', and a pink flowering cherry, such as *Prunus sargentii* 'Rancho', may be spectacular individually but they should never be brought together, as they so often are. In a small garden this may very well mean making a choice between one plant or the other.

Colors deepen as summer starts. There are numerous pinks among climbers, shrubs and trees, including clematis, crab apples (*Malus*), deutzia, the Judas tree (*Cercis siliquastrum*), kolkwitzia, Persian lilac (*Syringa × persica*) and weigela. Similar colors are picked up in plants on a smaller scale, such as alliums, border pinks, peonies, rock roses (*Helianthemum*) and valerian (*Centranthus ruber*). Blues include campanulas, delphiniums, irises, lithospermum and ceanothus, the latter among the best of the blue-flowered shrubs. Roses, too, start to bloom at this time in pinks, whites, yellows and reds.

There is a dramatic change as the summer progresses, the soft pinks and blues making way for warm reds, oranges and yellows, the red roses acting as a link between the two periods. Cannas, dahlia varieties such as 'Bishop of Llandaff', fuchsias, lilies, *Lobelia cardinalis*, oriental poppies, sweet bergamot (*Monarda didyma*) and verbena would make a stunning collection of red-flowered plants. Among the oranges are more lilies, climbers such as *Lonicera × tellmanniana* and the trumpet vine (*Campsis*), as well as numerous annuals and perennials, including alstroemerias, impatiens, montbretia,

This composition, climaxing in early summer, features pink aquilegia, hostas, geraniums, and border pinks in bud, with an apple tree behind.

Below: An early summer composition. White apple blossom and pale pink *Polygonum bistorta* have a softening effect on the stronger pink rhododendrons which could otherwise become overpowering, particularly in a small garden. The polygonum is long-flowering, and will carry on the color theme well after the rhododendrons have faded.

Center: In a large walled garden a romantic atmosphere is created all summer by an abundance of soft colors in tones of pink and mauve. In the foreground are purple and pink *Salvia horminum*, with hydrangea and *Echinops ritro* behind.

Far right: A pink geranium and purple-red iris complement each other in early summer. The iris will fade, leaving the geranium sustaining the color theme.

potentilla and an old stalwart of cottage gardens, the pot marigold. Yellows, at the end of the warm spectrum, include achilleas, California poppies (*Eschscholzia*), rudbeckia, ligularias, the monkey flower (*Mimulus*) and towering sunflowers. All these plants in related colors set the summer garden ablaze and stand up well to the heat and intensity of light before the days begin to draw in and become major color components of the garden.

Autumn flowers are somewhat neglected, but they extend the color season and for this are invaluable. Best among them are cimicifugas in white, monkshood (*Aconitum*) in blue, Michaelmas daisies in pink and purple, and nerines in pink and white. All of these go well together, but chrysanthemums in shades of yellow, coppery red and orange associate best with the foliage tints and fruits that color the autumn garden. The splendidly colored crops of barberries, cotoneasters, firethorns, flowering crabs, hawthorns, hollies, mountain ash and euonymus show to good effect against evergreen foliage.

It is important to identify from the outset the color scheme you want and then to stick to it. This requires a certain amount of discipline. I, for one, am frequently tempted to include a new plant just because I have an urge to grow it, but this is the first step on the slippery road to a spotty effect: I often find that my new plant has to be moved.

Using a restrained palette makes it easier to build up a coherent composition and to create a restful picture. The skill then lies in finding plant associations that take the color scheme through the year. My advice is to begin with just two or three colors as the basis for your initial schemes. This way, you have plenty of scope for experiment without the results becoming too complicated.

Below: **A cool composition of plants with bluish tints make a late-spring picture in a shady spot. The tall pink spikes of** *Polygonum bistorta* **are the focal point, with magenta** *Primula* **and blue forget-me-nots edging the bed. The white geranium introduces some light. The primulas will disappear first, followed by the forget-me-nots. The polygonum will then continue for another month, outlasted by the geraniums.**

Opposite page, left: *Geranium* **'Johnson's Blue' is a useful ground-covering perennial that grows well in sun or light shade. The flowers, which appear in late spring, will last for a month in shade, less in sun.**

Opposite page, center: **The glaucous foliage of this wallflower,** *Erysimum* **'Bowles' Mauve', would have a strong impact on a blue spring border, together with, for example, forget-me-nots, pulmonaria and omphalodes. It can be in flower for most of the year.**
Opposite page, right: *Anchusa azurea* **has the characteristic blue flowers (early summer) of the borage family.**

Some examples will speak more eloquently than theory. If you decide on a combination of pink and mauve, there is a host of different plants to choose from. You could design a summer flower border around these colors with *Heuchera*, *Sedum* 'Autumn Joy', border pinks and dwarf lavender in front of geraniums (*G. endressii* and *G. sanguineum*), *Lilium regale*, penstemons and *Lavatera* 'Barnsley'. A few gray-

you could juxtapose blue and yellow, combining pulmonaria and daffodils, brunnera, forget-me-not and the yellow tulip 'West Point'. Later the yellows could give way to pinks, with the blues of comfrey, irises and lithospermum combining with dianthus and alliums, and columbines adding their contribution to both colors. If the pinks are supplemented with whites, the blues will appear clearer. Delphiniums and campan-

try a combination of yellow, red and orange. The celebrated Edwardian gardener, Gertrude Jekyll, whose book *Colour Schemes for the Flower Garden* has had a powerful influence on the handling of color in 20th-century gardens, proposed a scheme using these three colors. She suggested orange dahlias, african marigolds, rudbeckia and helenium linking scarlet salvias, dahlias, lilies and lychnis

leaved plants, such as *Stachys olympica*, *Artemisia* 'Powis Castle' and *A. ludoviciana*, will enhance the soft colors. An ideal backdrop to this scheme would be a wall or trellis panel supporting roses such as the pink 'Aloha' and the paler 'Climbing Cécile Brunner' combined with pink or mauve clematis, such as 'Nelly Moser' or 'Hagley Hybrid'.

You might try designing a composition based on plants with blue flowers, as these associate well with flowers in a variety of other colors. The blue could run as a year-long theme throughout the flower border, or you could pair blue with other colors. For example, for a striking contrast in spring

ulas come in blues and whites, sweet peas and tobacco plant, astrantia and lilies in pink and white.

To intensify the blue you could introduce purple in place of white. For summer you could use catmint (*Nepeta*), *Salvia* 'Superba', geraniums, *Phlox paniculata* and statice (*Limonium*). Autumn-flowering plants might include monkshood (*Aconitum*) and asters. And to finish the year in blue triumph there are few better plants than *Ceratostigma plumbaginoides*.

These examples already show how much scope the gardener has when working in three rather than two colors. To give a vivid impression in late summer you might

with warm yellow french marigolds, helianthus, coreopsis, achillea and buphthalmum.

A spring version of the same colors could include the orange tulip 'General de Wet', red, orange and yellow wallflowers and pansies, dark purple-red *Bergenia* 'Abendglut' (which has bronze foliage), orange *Euphorbia griffithii* 'Fire Glow' and *Geum borisii*.

A less usual but attractive combination would be purple, bronzy orange and silver. I vividly recall seeing this in a planting that included dark purple *Sedum telephium maximum* 'Atropurpureum' growing next to the so-called pheasant's-tail grass (*Stipa arundinacea*). This is a striking plant in late summer, when its arching leaves are bronze with a hint of orange and red, and the deeper color was brought out by the dark foliage of the sedum. With these were the silver *Artemisia canescens*, bronzy-leaved *Crocosmia* 'Solfatare', which also has flowers tinged apricot, a self-sown spike of red-leaved orach (*Atriplex hortensis* 'Rubra'), *Digitalis ferruginea*, which has orange-brown and white flowers, and the purple mullein (*Verbascum phoeniceum*), which has white flowers with a purple eye.

Within each combination of two or three colors there are always tonal variations that will give substance and depth to the scheme. To make the most of these it is advisable to group plants in drifts so that there are no abrupt transitions of color.

Although many color-schemes begin with the choice of a color or combination of colors, another starting point is a favorite plant. I am particularly fond of the different hellebores. The lenten rose (*Helleborus orientalis*), which flowers in early spring, has many hybrids, the colors ranging from creamy white to deep purple. Those tending to purple look beautiful under the pale yellow *Corylopsis pauciflora* or simply with lemon-yellow daffodils. The stinking hellebore (*H. foetidus*) has green flowers and dark gray-green leaves that make a vivid contrast with the red stems of *Cornus alba* 'Sibirica'. These are plants around which I would happily develop more complex color schemes.

Clematis also rank high among my favorite plants, and basing a color composition around a well-chosen variety is a popular and worthwhile approach. On a recent visit to a garden I was much struck by the simple combination of the mauve-blue flowers of *Clematis* 'Perle d'Azur' with the gray-purple foliage of *Rosa glauca* through which it was growing. Roses and clematis are particularly successful companions. The clematis can complement or contrast with the rose when it is in flower, and extend its season by flowering either before or after it.

In this way a shrub or climbing rose can be full of interest from late spring right through to the autumn, especially if it also produces hips.

It is best to choose a large-flowered clematis for a clematis-rose partnership. The clematis can be pruned hard back in early spring so that it does not conflict with the rose in terms of pruning routine and will not be so vigorous that it will swamp its support. By hard pruning early-flowering varieties (which normally are cut back only lightly) their flowering can be delayed to coincide with the rose's period in bloom. There are some particularly successful clematis-rose partnerships: the early-flowering red clematis 'Niobe' just precedes the hybrid perpetual deep red rose 'Souvenir du Docteur Jamain'; the later purple 'Jackmanii Superba' coincides with the yellow climbing rose 'Golden Showers'; and the late-flowering lilac clematis 'Madame Baron-Veillard' extends the season of the similarly colored hybrid tea rose 'Blue Moon'. Rosy-purple 'Victoria' contrasts well with the yellow-flowered *Rosa* 'Royal Gold'.

Clematis go well with many other summer-flowering shrubs. The purple starry flowers of 'Lasurstern' look beautiful with the clean white "snowball" flowers of *Viburnum opulus* 'Roseum'. Wine red *Clematis* 'Madame Julia Correvon' extends the season of reddy-pink *Kolkwitzia amabilis*. In a purple scheme the small white and mauve flowers of *C. viticella* 'Minuet' make a happy marriage with the purple-red leaves of *Cotinus coggygria* 'Foliis Purpureis'.

Clematis also look good growing through shrubs that have a short but glorious

Above: **The electric impact of these purple and vermilion primulas (*P. pulverulenta*) is heightened by harmonizing rhododendrons that flower at the same time – late spring. Both these plants like moist, acid conditions.**

Above right: In this composition, *Helenium autumnale* is accompanied by orange lilies and yellow alstroemerias. In late summer, the helenium has just come into flower, picking up the color baton from orange poppies that are just fading.

Right: *Helenium autumnale*, in early autumn. Bright orange crocosmia would make a suitable partner. Both are long-lasting in their flowering.

Above: Different shades of green and white make a tasteful combination in this small group of plants in the shade, seen at the beginning of spring. Snowdrops and *Helleborus corsicus* with white and pale green flowers combine with the dark green leaves of the hellebore and variegated leaves of *Arum italicum* 'Pictum' (jack-in-the-pulpit): the latter will develop red berries in late summer.
Right: The golden variegated form of *Iris pallida*, with scented blue flowers in early summer, makes a strong vertical counterpoint to the soft feathery foliage of yellow-flowering *Meconopsis cambrica*. The colors are complementary but the textures contrasting.

flowering season. This is particularly true of winter and early-spring shrubs that tend to have little to commend them once their flowering is over. Try rosy-mauve 'Hagley Hybrid' through *Forsythia suspensa*, or white 'Marie Boisselot' through *Lonicera fragrantissima*.

Allowing clematis to thread their way through other climbers, particularly against walls, is another successful way to grow them. *Cotoneaster horizontalis* grown against a shady wall is the perfect host for the early flowering *Clematis macropetala*. The blue clematis is followed in summer by the snowy white flowers of the cotoneaster, which are followed in autumn by red berries. In spring it is not always possible to predict whether *C. montana* 'Rubens' will flower with or after the early Dutch honeysuckle (*Lonicera periclymenum* 'Belgica'), but when flowering coincides the combination of colors (pinks and pale yellow) and the blending of perfumes delight the senses. Another attractive combination for a warm wall is the variegated ivy *Hedera canariensis* 'Gloire de Marengo' and *C.* 'Henryi'.

It is in winter that I particularly enjoy working out color duos and trios, dreaming up compositions that sometimes verge on the eccentric. For example, I have had an idea for a "chic" black and white scheme: an edging of the black lily turf (*Ophiopogon planiscapus* 'Nigrescens') with the black tulip 'Queen of the Night' and the white lily-flowered tulip 'White Triumphator', rising from a bed of silver-leaved and white-flowered snow-in-summer (*Cerastium tomentosum*), with self-sown black *Viola* 'Bowles Black' here and there. This must remain a dream as I cannot find a place to implement the scheme. There are, however, countless other exciting combinations that I could realistically plant – far more than I am ever likely to be able to put into effect.

Left: In early summer, white variegated honesty contrasts with pink wild carrot.
Below, left: In this summer composition, the rather acid yellow of the kniphofias has a brightening effect on the ageing golden yellow flowers of the achillea. The differing shapes of the blooms give an additional dimension to the picture created.
Below: Tall purple allium adds brightness and distinction to the golden variegated foliage of lemon balm (*Melissa officinalis* 'Aurea') and box (*Buxus sempervirens* 'Aureovariegata'), whose tightly clipped shape stands out against the feathery foliage of sweet cicely. The composition, pictured in early summer, looks very striking against the mature yew hedge.

An all-white garden has a very restful effect on the eye but needs strong lines to be successful.

Right: Delphiniums, lilies, loosestrife and violets make a solid bank of white at the height of summer.

This page, below: In high summer, the soft forms of a white *Limnanthes douglasii* and white variegated comfrey and hosta are counterpointed by the sword-shaped iris leaves.

Far right: The delicate pale gray foliage of *Argyranthemum frutescens* delicately offsets the lovely daisy-like flowers. This plant, which is tender and flowers through the summer, could be combined successfully with other white-flowering plants, or it could act as a foil or background for stronger colors.

FRAMEWORK AND FOLIAGE

There are plenty of flowers to provide a year-long succession of color, but a garden that relies exclusively on flowers neglects a major plant resource. Foliage, infinitely varied in color, shape and texture as well as in the manner in which it is carried, should be one of the most important elements in the design and planting of a garden. Whether as formal hedges and lawns or as a looser planting of trees, shrubs, climbers and perennials, it creates the green backcloth of a garden. However, this is far from being the only importance of foliage, for the leaves of many plants are just as effective as flowers in providing striking and beautiful details in the garden.

In comparison with the ephemeral beauty of flowers and fruit, foliage is a relatively stable feature of the garden, yet it is constantly changing through the seasons. Evergreens provide the link between the old and new years, but their color is far from uniform from month to month. Many conifers, for example, show a marked change as new growth starts. The new buds of some yews are rusty-ocher, while those of others are pale green. The blue junipers are surrounded by growth of pale fluffiness that deepens in color and firms up through the summer.

It is, however, with deciduous plants that seasonal changes are most pronounced. Most trees and shrubs have definite phases, which can be divided into bud burst, full canopy, autumn color and leaf fall. In spring there are the delicate tints and fresh greens of unfurling leaves. By summer, leaves develop to fill every available space, mingling in color and texture with the evergreens. When the canopies of trees and shrubs are full, there is a deeper toning in the multitude of shades. The pace of change quickens again with autumn, plants standing out from one another more sharply as their leaves take on gloriously rich colors. And then, for several months, the gaunt silhouettes of deciduous trees and shrubs, together with colored and variegated evergreens, and plants with attractive barks, stand out against the dark greens of plants such as holly and yew.

The timetable for deciduous plants is far from uniform, some starting their cycle well before others. Among trees, willows and balsam poplars are some of the earliest into leaf. The horse chestnut is early too, and among the first to shed its leaves, followed by beech and sycamore. Ash comes into leaf very late, and the leaves drop all at once after the first frost.

In some cases the color changes throughout the year can be extraordinarily subtle. For example, the golden false acacia (*Robinia pseudoacacia* 'Frisia'), comes into leaf very late. At first the growth is palest green, and shortly after seems to stop, and one wonders if the plant will survive. However, a month later, as summer gets into swing, the leaves reach full size and the tree assumes a soft billowy appearance of nearly translucent yellowy green, which glows against clear blue and overcast skies alike. As summer progresses, the color alters imperceptibly, but when some leaves turn a distinct yellow there is a two-tone effect. By autumn the whole tree is a soft butter-yellow, and the leaves thin out until a narrow twiggy gray silhouette is left for the winter.

The example of the robinia is a reminder of the considerable color range that can be found in foliage. Apart from every shade of green, from near-blues to near-yellows, there are palest grays and darkest mauvy

In late spring the fresh young foliage of herbaceous plants has a delicate beauty that is unequaled at any other time of year. Prominent here are the strap-shaped leaves of day lilies and the feathery fronds of fennel.

Right: The warm russet colors of autumn leaves are one of the highlights of the year for many trees and shrubs. Maple and mountain ash are the main elements in this corner of a woodland garden. The mountain ash, which flowers in early summer, is here seen with its red berries.

Opposite: Variegated hostas and ferns present foliage textures in a sunken shady garden. In such a site you need to rely heavily on foliage for summer interest, although here there are foxgloves in bloom to add points of color.

blacks, as well as many examples with golden yellow or variegated foliage. This last group includes conifers with cream variegations, such as *Thujopsis dolabrata* 'Variegata' and *Chamaecyparis lawsoniana* 'Albospica', and golden forms of cypresses, yew, junipers and arborvitae. These are all useful alternatives to the solid green forms, introducing variety to color schemes and changing very markedly with light. Many broadleaved shrubs, both evergreen and deciduous, also have variegated and golden forms. The evergreen, recently introduced *Choisya ternata* 'Sundance' and the deciduous *Philadelphus coronarius* 'Aureus' both make a golden splash of foliage. Yellow, cream and white variegation that provides light relief in shady corners is particularly good in species of hollies, elaeagnus, cornus, euonymus and weigela.

The range of foliage color allows scope for color compositions with or without flowers. Yellow foliage and flowers and golden variegated forms will be highlighted when planted beside purple plants such as the purple smoke bush (*Cotinus coggygria* 'Notcutt's Variety') or a purple-leaved New Zealand flax, the wonderfully architectural *Phormium tenax* 'Purpureum'. Gray foliage, for example that of artemisias and santolinas, is especially useful for cooling bedding schemes that include what might otherwise be strident pinks, reds and purples. A combination that to my mind is particularly tasteful, gray and purple, could be composed entirely of foliage. A fine association would consist of a rounded bush of the purple hazel (*Corylus maxima* 'Purpurea') below a huge-leaved whitebeam, *Sorbus latifolia* 'Mitchellii', with support from *Rosa glauca*, with rosy-gray leaves, and *Phormium tenax* 'Sundowner', the latter having tall spikes of grayish purple and creamy white.

From the last example alone it will be clear that color is not the only leaf characteristic that needs to be taken into account when placing plants in the garden. Shapes vary from minute needles to enormous heart shapes and parasols. In some plants the edges are even, as in the bergenias; in others, such as the alchemillas, delicately frilled; and in others again, dramatically jagged, as in the tender melianthus. The texture of foliage varies enormously, too. Some leaves, such as those of the camellias, are smooth and

shiny; many are matt; yet others, for example on the pasqueflower (*Pulsatilla vulgaris*), are downy or hairy.

The individuality of a plant is also a matter of how the leaves are carried. They may look like upright swords, as with the phormiums; they can be closely set, in a way that makes box, for example, such a good hedging plant; they can be light and airy, as with some ferns; and they can be stiff and unyielding, in the way that makes some of the thistles so bold and distinctive.

A collection of plants of undifferentiated leaf size, shape and texture is just as likely to be an amorphous mess as a planting in a single color. It is particularly important in mixed borders, clothed with perennials but with a backbone of shrubs, to take account of all the attributes of leaves, arriving at a

balance between plants of very different characteristics. It helps if for every stage of the year there is a plant that because of its foliage puts its stamp on the site, giving it an unmistakable identity.

Epimediums and hostas are outstanding examples of the many perennials that are grown principally for their leaves. A superb border in which flowers hardly feature can be made using these and similar plants. However, it should not be thought that there are no good flowering perennials with attractive foliage. Achilleas, bear's breeches (*Acanthus*), *Brunnera macrophylla*, candytuft (*Iberis*), hellebores, ligularias and peonies are just a few of the many that are valued for their flowers but which in addition have good foliage through the growing season.

Hedges and lawns, both key elements in the structure of a garden, change with the seasons, even dramatically, as in the case of deciduous hedges of beech and hornbeam. It is, however, their regular shapes and forms and relatively uniform color that gives point to the less restrained shapes and hues of ornamental planting. In general, the more simply lawns and hedges are treated, the more effective they will be as foils for exuberant borders or other features such as ornaments or statues. Where elements in the garden's framework have a marked pattern or detail of their own – a tapestry hedge, for example, made of more than one species, or a lawn mown with contrasting areas of long and short grass – it is probably best to treat the accompanying planting very plainly.

Although there is an increasing interest in foliage plants and an awareness of the role foliage can play in the garden, it is surprising the extent to which many gardeners are still so mesmerized by flowers that they neglect this major component almost completely.

FRAGRANCE

Before I had my own garden I always knew that, in principle, plants with scent should have a prior claim to garden space. However, I did not then fully appreciate the pleasure that fragrant and aromatic plants can give through all the seasons of the year. Now that I have experienced that pleasure to the full, I recognize the difficulty of writing about it. Although the literature of all periods is full of references expressing delight in scented plants, there is in effect a very limited vocabulary to describe specific fragrances. For lack of it, scents that are assumed to be familiar are used as points of reference. The flowers of *Cytisus battandieri* are said to smell like pineapple, those of *Magnolia grandiflora* are described as lemon-scented, the sweet briar (*Rosa rubiginosa*) is claimed to have an apple fragrance, while *Thymus comosus* is generally likened to turpentine.

Sensitivity to smell varies from individual to individual, some people picking up fragrances that completely elude others. Just as unpredictable are individual reactions to scents; what delights one person may seem sickly or offensive to another. Our reactions are no doubt deeply influenced by the associations that a smell triggers off but they are not always easy to fathom. I dislike intensely the garlicky smell of *Phuopsis stylosa* (which reminds me of drunks on the early-morning Paris metro), but I am fascinated by the strong curry smell of *Helichrysum italicum*; yet I am fond of garlic, in moderation, and dislike a strong curry.

The variations of scent within the plant world can be as mysterious as human reactions to it. Different forms of a single species can show marked variations in the intensity of perfume. Not all *Clematis montana*, for example, have the distinctive vanilla-like fragrance of some forms. Plant breeding to improve flower size and

Above: **A sunny dry patch in the garden is the ideal spot for a herb garden filled with pungent aromatics. The curry plant (*Helichrysum italicum*), thyme, marjoram and sage all combine here to create a complex fragrance with Mediterranean overtones.**
Right: *Lilium regale* **is a summer-flowering bulb. Each stem may produce up to twenty-five trumpet-shaped scented flowers that will fill a garden with their perfume.**

form has resulted in many instances in a loss of fragrance. Sweet peas, carnations and roses are all plants traditionally thought of as highly scented but many modern varieties are almost or completely scentless. The revival of "old-fashioned" flowers is to some extent reversing this trend.

Climatic conditions and time of day are among factors affecting the strength of scents emitted by flowers. In general, the warmer the conditions, the stronger the scent. Although summer scents are generally the strongest and headiest, some winter- and spring-flowering plants, including *Viburnum farreri* and *Chimonanthus praecox*, have particularly powerful fragrances. Some flowers, such as those of the shrubby honeysuckle (*Lonicera fragrantissima*) and *Corylopsis spicata*, only show their full strength when brought into a warm room. While most rose flowers smell best with the sun on them, it takes a shower of rain to bring out the rich foliage scent of the sweet briar. The scents of some flowers are detectable only in the evening. There is the light fragrance of the aptly named evening primrose (*Oenothera missourensis* or *O. odorata*), and the heavier note of the night-scented stock (*Matthiola bicornis*), which during the day seems to have such insignificant flowers. Bouncing bet (*Saponaria officinalis*), a robust and unruly plant, also emits a heavy evening fragrance, which some might find sickly. Prettier than any of these is the tobacco plant, and the perfume it diffuses in the evening is delicious. The wild species, *Nicotiana alata*, is the best of several tobacco plants; in mild climates it is perennial and it grows to a sensible height, nearly 4 feet (1.2m), for its scent to be enjoyed at close quarters.

Aromatic plants, with scented leaves, stems and even roots, add a spicy note to the fragrant garden. Many are culinary herbs but in some cases the scent of their leaves would be enough to justify a place in the plot. The scent of some is released freely but others oblige only when they are brushed against or crushed. Among herbaceous aromatic plants that die down in winter are artemisia, monarda, fennel, lovage and mint. The evergreens include sage, santolina, sweet bay, rosemary, thyme and winter savory. Many of these plants are of Mediterranean origin and are slightly tender. To enjoy evergreens throughout the year it is a good idea to grow them in pots that can be brought in during hard winters.

The smells and fragrances of each season are distinctive, and it is worth planting a garden to make the most of the natural sequence. In spring there are fresh crisp smells to match the new growth unfurling all round. Jonquils and *Narcissus* 'Cheerfulness' strike the right note, and perhaps these could be combined with wallflowers to make a scented bed backed by the evergreen *Osmanthus delavayi*, daphne and *Skimmia japonica*. To follow there are cowslips, lily-of-the-valley and, my favorite of all, *Viburnum carlesii*.

In summer I think of freshly cut grass and the strong fragrance of wisteria, lilacs, mock orange and the allspice (*Calycanthus floridus*). It is the season, too, for honeysuckles, lilies, phlox and pinks, all of which are scented flowers that have long been in cultivation. And then there are roses, which should always be selected with scent in mind. Among the hybrid teas, 'Wendy Cussons', 'Alec's Red' and 'Mister Lincoln' all have rich red velvety flowers with perfumes to match. For some the old-fashioned roses will always be the first choice – 'La Reine Victoria', 'Madame Isaac Pereire', 'Souvenir de la Malmaison'.

The fallen leaves of autumn smell damp and musty, but those of *Cercidiphyllum japonicum* I associate with the aroma of toasted marshmallow. The late-flowering pepper bush (*Clethra alnifolia*), *Clerodendron trichotomum* and *Perovskia* 'Blue Spire' produce a lingering spiciness.

On a clear crisp day in winter there are flowers to please the nose as well as the eye. Among the bulbs there are crocuses (*C. laevigatus* and *C. chrysanthus*), snowdrops (*Galanthus nivalis* and *G. elwesii*) and irises (*I. reticulata* and *I. unguicularis*). The Chinese witch hazel (*Hamamelis mollis*) can look startling when covered with its spidery fragrant flowers. Although the flowers of *Lonicera fragrantissima*, *Elaeagnus macrophylla* and *Azara microphylla* are insignificant, their sweet scent makes them especially welcome in the coldest months.

To give full value, fragrant and aromatic plants need to be well placed and this is especially true for those plants that can only be enjoyed at close range. A sunny position against a warm wall is an ideal spot for many, as there they will release their scent freely.

THE SEASONAL GARDEN

A rewarding approach to gardening is to plan for a climax of interest in one season, providing extra support at other times of year from foliage, flowers and fruit. The setting for such a climax is traditionally the border. For many gardeners the creation of a rich border, designed to show off harmonious effects of color and texture, is the ultimate ambition.

The first stage in creating a border is to draw up a plan, taking the flowering and foliage characteristics of the plants into account, as well as heights and contours. There are two basic ways of planting, in clumps or in drifts. You need to bear in mind the ultimate spread of each plant, and estimate the number of plants accordingly. It is unwise to plant more perennials than you need, and then remove them periodically to make space for growth, as this will produce an unnatural, unbalanced effect. The best strategy is to plant exactly what you need for the future, and fill the gaps with annuals initially.

Autumn or spring are the best times for planting. A spring border will need to be planted the previous autumn. Acquire all the plants you need, so that you can plant in a single session.

Adequate soil preparation is essential. Perennial weeds must be eradicated, even if this means leaving the ground fallow for a season. Before planting, place the plants on the ground in their planned positions, and make any adjustments you judge necessary.

At the time of planting, extra nutrients should be incorporated around the plants, and a light mulch applied. Plant bulbs deep, and to avoid the risk of digging them up accidentally, mark their position with a

Opposite: A beautiful composition in late summer, featuring the grass *Stipa arundinacea*; in the autumn this will be enhanced by pendent open panicles of purplish green flower spikes. To the left is *Sedum* 'Autumn Joy', which produces dense heads of coral-pink starry flowers in late summer and autumn.

label, stick or sprinkle of sand. Such reminders can make all the difference.

The setting of a planting scheme needs to be taken into account when planning seasonal color effects. For example, there is no better background for a mixture of white flowers and gray foliage than the dark green of a yew or a holly hedge. A red border could look splendid against a hedge of ordinary beech, although it would not be so successful against copper beech.

The following pages look at some specific ideas for particular seasons of the year. First are three planting "programs" for spring, summer and autumn borders. Although these borders have been carefully contrived to climax in one particular season, suggestions for extending the season are also provided, together with ideas for creating "interim" interest in the first year, before the border has had time to fully establish itself. Each program is followed by a flowering and maintenance chart, which covers the interim planting as well as the main planting. (For advice on mulching, see p. 150.)

Note that all subjects listed in the charts have been planted the previous autumn, unless otherwise stated. Some annuals, such as *Viola odora* and *Chelidonium*, will self-sow successfully. Others that self-sow, such as aquilegias, will in time revert to their wild form and in the process will become less vigorous and less showy; such plants need to be weeded out in spring and, as indicated in the charts, resown from new seed.

For an earlier display, half-hardy and tender annuals such as petunias and sweet peas can be sown in early spring in heat (see the chart on p. 129).

PROGRAM FOR A SPRING BORDER

A *First year, spring*   B *The border in summer*

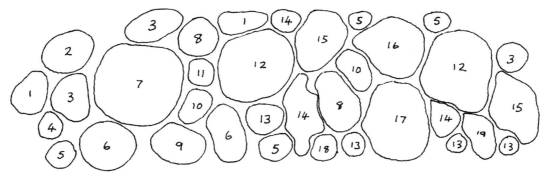

The ideal place to have a spring border is a site that is light but sheltered. The border illustrated here, created at the base of a flowering cherry, contains a collection of classic spring plants that includes bulbs and perennials. A euphorbia (12) and juniper (16) give height and continuity.

During the first year (A) the number of bulbs can be increased and supplemented by wallflowers in a sea of forget-me-not. Daisies, pansies and small bulbs such as *Ipheion* 'Wisley Blue' would make a suitable edging.

In summer (B) perennials take over from the bulbs, the dominant plants being foxgloves (11), catmint (17), day lilies (7) and *Lavatera* (2). The campanulas and catmint harmonize effectively with the glaucous foliage of the euphorbia and juniper.

1 *Meconopsis betonicifolia*
2 *Lavatera*
3 *Aquilegia*
4 *Viola cornuta*
5 *Primula vulgaris*
6 *Helleborus orientalis*
7 *Hemerocallis*
8 Tulips
9 *Bergenia*
10 *Campanula*
11 *Digitalis purpurea*
12 *Euphorbia characias wulfenii*
13 *Stachys macrantha*
14 Daffodils
15 *Tulipa* 'Apeldorn'
16 *Juniperus* 'Skyrocket'
17 *Nepeta* × *faassenii*
18 Fern
19 *Heuchera* × *brizoides*

SPRING BORDER: *FLOWERING AND MAINTENANCE*

KEY:

SOW ▫	DIVIDE ⬆	CUTTINGS 🌱
STAKE I	PRUNE ✂	FOLIAGE ▨
PLANT 🌰	DEADHEAD ✂	FLOWERS ▨
LIFT ▲	PICK ⚘	FRUIT ▨

	FIRST YEAR									THIRD YEAR
	EARLY SPRING	MID SPRING	LATE SPRING	EARLY SUMMER	MID SUMMER	LATE SUMMER	EARLY AUTUMN	LATE AUTUMN	WINTER	**Plants to lift and divide in autumn**
1 *Meconopsis betonicifolia*						sow				
2 *Lavatera*	prune									
3 *Aquilegia*	sow							deadhead		
4 *Viola cornuta*										
5 *Primula vulgaris*		deadhead	deadhead							
6 *Helleborus orientalis*										
7 *Hemerocallis*						deadhead				divide
8 Tulips			deadhead	deadhead	lift		plant	plant		
9 *Bergenia*			deadhead	deadhead						
10 *Campanula*					deadhead	deadhead				
11 *Digitalis purpurea*					deadhead					
12 *Euphorbia characias wulfenii*										divide
13 *Stachys macrantha*										
14 Daffodils		deadhead	deadhead				plant	plant		
15 *Tulipa* 'Apeldorn'			deadhead		lift		plant	plant		
16 *Juniperus* 'Skyrocket'										
17 *Nepeta* x *faassenii*							deadhead			
18 Fern										
19 *Heuchera* x *brizoides*	prune									
	INTERIM PLANTING									
Pansies				plant						
Myosotis (forget-me-not)				plant						
Wallflowers				plant						
Bellis perennis (daisies)				plant						
Ipheion uniflorum 'Wisley Blue'										
Tulipa 'West Point'					plant					

PROGRAM FOR A SUMMER BORDER

A First year, summer

B The border in spring

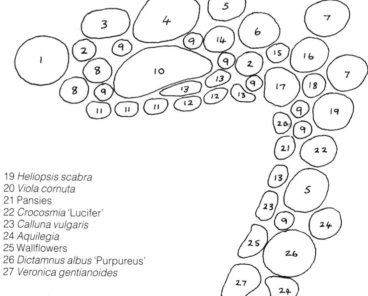

The summer border illustrated has a broad color theme including pinks and white, with some touches of warm red, orange and yellow.

In the first year (A) annuals in shades to match the long-term planting could be used to fill out the border. For example, pink sweet peas and *Rudbeckia* Giant Hybrids would give height at the back of the border. Plants for the middle and front include cosmos, baby's breath, mesembryanthemum, petunias, stock and night-scented stock.

In spring (B), when the perennials are just appearing, daffodils, tulips and crown imperials herald the warm colors of the summer.

1 Rose 'Marguerite Hilling'
2 *Helleborus orientalis*
3 *Clematis* 'Gipsy Queen' through rose 'Crimson Rambler'
4 *Lythrum salicaria*
5 *Achillea* ('Gold Plate', 'Salmon Beauty')
6 *Rudbeckia* 'Goldsturm'
7 *Phlox* 'Norah Leigh'
8 *Chelidonium majus*
9 Tulips

10 *Osteospermum ecklonis*
11 *Dianthus* 'Brympton Red'
12 *Dianthus* 'Enid Anderson'
13 *Viola ordora*
14 *Penstemon* 'Firebird'
15 *Geum*
16 *Malva moschata*
17 *Sedum* 'Autumn Joy'
18 *Ligularia* 'The Rocket'

19 *Heliopsis scabra*
20 *Viola cornuta*
21 Pansies
22 *Crocosmia* 'Lucifer'
23 *Calluna vulgaris*
24 *Aquilegia*
25 Wallflowers
26 *Dictamnus albus* 'Purpureus'
27 *Veronica gentianoides*

SUMMER BORDER: *FLOWERING AND MAINTENANCE*

KEY:

SOW ☐	DIVIDE ⬆⬆	CUTTINGS 🌱
STAKE |	PRUNE ✄	FOLIAGE (shade)
PLANT ⬎	DEADHEAD ✂	FLOWER (shade)
LIFT ▲	PICK ↓	FRUIT (shade)

		FIRST YEAR									THIRD YEAR
		EARLY SPRING	MID SPRING	LATE SPRING	EARLY SUMMER	MID SUMMER	LATE SUMMER	EARLY AUTUMN	LATE AUTUMN	WINTER	Plants to lift and divide in autumn
1	Rose 'Marguerite Hilling'									✄	
2	*Helleborus orientalis*										
3	*Clematis* 'Gipsy Queen'	✄									
4	*Lythrum salicaria*							✂	✂		⬆⬆
5	*Achillea* ('Gold Plate', 'Salmon Beauty')			(shade)	(shade)			✂	✂		⬆⬆
6	*Rudbeckia* 'Goldsturm'							✂	✂		⬆⬆
7	*Phlox* 'Norah Leigh'			(shade)	(shade)			✂	✂		⬆⬆
8	*Chelidonium majus*										
9	Tulips			✂	✂			⬎	⬎		
10	*Osteospermum ecklonis*					✂	✂	✂			⬆⬆
11	*Dianthus* 'Brympton Red'		(shade)	(shade)		✂	✂	🌱			
12	*Dianthus* 'Enid Anderson'		(shade)	(shade)		✂	✂	🌱			
13	*Viola ordora*										
14	*Penstemon* 'Firebird'						✂	✂			⬆⬆
15	*Geum*			(shade)		✂	✂	(shade)			⬆⬆
16	*Malva moschata*							🌱			
17	*Sedum* 'Autumn Joy'	✄		(shade)							
18	*Ligularia* 'The Rocket'						✂	✂	✂		
19	*Heliopsis scabra*						✂	✂	✂		
20	*Viola cornuta*										
21	Pansies	(shade)						⬎			
22	*Crocosmia* 'Lucifer'				(shade)	(shade)					⬆⬆
23	*Calluna vulgaris*							✄			
24	*Aquilegia*	☐					(shade)	(shade)	✂		
25	Wallflowers					☐					
26	*Dictamnus albus* 'Purpureus'					✂					
27	*Veronica gentianoides*					✂	✂				
	INTERIM PLANTING										
	Mentellia aurea	☐						▲			
	Cosmos	☐	☐	☐ ⬎			✂	▲			
	Mesembryenthemum	☐		⬎			✂	▲			
	Night-scented stock	☐	☐	☐				▲			
	Petunia	☐		⬎		✂	✂	▲			
	Rudbeckia 'Giant Hybrids'	☐	☐	☐			✂	✂	▲		
	Tithonia 'Goldfinger'	☐		⬎			✂	✂	▲		
	Sweet peas	☐	☐	⬎		↓	↓	▲			
	Stock	☐	☐	☐ ⬎			✂	▲			
	Helichrysum monstrosum	☐	☐	☐				↓			
	Gypsophila elegans 'Alba'	☐	☐	☐		↓	↓		▲		
	Verbena	☐					✂	✂	▲		
	Fritillaria imperialis			✂	✂						
	Daffodils	✂	✂	✂				⬎	⬎		
	Species tulips		✂	✂							
	Hybrid tulips			✂	✂	▲		⬎	⬎		
	Chionodoxa luciliae										

PROGRAM FOR AN AUTUMN BORDER

A *First year*

B *The border in late spring*

A

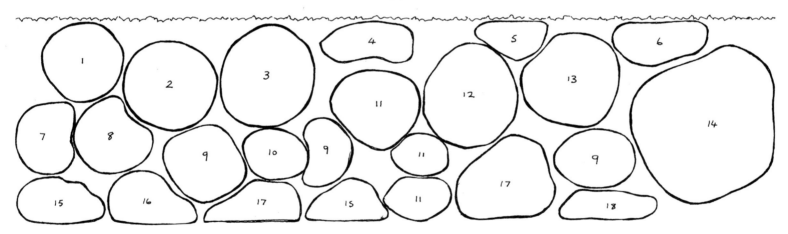

This border, backed by a beech hedge, looks most dramatic in autumn when the maroon foliage of the two barberries (3, 13) is at its deepest and matched by the flowers of the sedum (9).

During the first year (A) annuals and tender plants, including the gray-leaved *Senecio maritima*, the purple-leaved *Hibiscus* tone', burgundy-flowered *Amaranthus caudatus* and yellow dahlias, complement the permanent planting.

In late spring (B) the shrubby peony (14) and the two barberries are in full bloom, while the foreground is furnished with the evergreen mounds and white flowers of arabis (15, 17).

A Beech hedge
1 *Oenothera* 'Fireworks'
2 *Kniphofia* 'Buttercup'
3 *Berberis thunbergii* 'Atropurpurea'
4 *Rudbeckia* 'Autumn Sun'
5 *Coreopsis grandiflora*
6 *Genista aetnensis*
7 *Crocosmia* 'Firebird'
8 *Anaphalis triplinervis*
9 *Sedum* 'Autumn Joy'
10 *Santolina chamaecyparissus*
11 *Sisyrinchium striatum*

12 *Potentilla fruticosa* 'Elizabeth'
13 *Berberis* × *ottawensis* 'Purpurea'
14 *Paeonia lutea ludlowii*
15 *Arabis caucasica*
16 *Potentilla alba*
17 *Arabis caucasica* 'Flore Pleno'
18 *Santolina virens*

AUTUMN: *FLOWERING AND MAINTENANCE*

KEY:					
SOW	☐	DIVIDE	(divide symbol)	CUTTINGS	(cuttings symbol)
STAKE	I	PRUNE	(prune symbol)	FOLIAGE	(shading)
PLANT	(plant symbol)	DEADHEAD	(scissors)	FLOWER	(shading)
LIFT	(lift symbol)	PICK	(pick symbol)	FRUIT	(shading)

	FIRST YEAR									THIRD YEAR
	EARLY SPRING	MID SPRING	LATE SPRING	EARLY SUMMER	MID SUMMER	LATE SUMMER	EARLY AUTUMN	LATE AUTUMN	WINTER	Plants to lift and divide in autumn
A Beech hedge						Prune				
1 *Oenothera* 'Fireworks'					Deadhead	Deadhead				
2 *Kniphofia* 'Buttercup'										
3 *Berberis thunbergii* 'Atropurpurea'									Prune	
4 *Rudbeckia* 'Autumn Sun'										Divide
5 *Coreopsis grandiflora*										
6 *Genista aethnensis*										
7 *Crocosmia* 'Firebird'										
8 *Anaphalis triplinervis*										
9 *Sedum* 'Autumn Joy'	Prune									
10 *Santolina chamaecyparissus*	Prune				Deadhead	Deadhead				
11 *Sisyrinchium striatum*					Deadhead					Divide
12 Potentilla fruticosa 'Elizabeth'	Prune									
13 *Berberis* x *ottawensis* 'Purpurea'									Prune	
14 *Paeonia lutea ludlowii*								Prune		
15 *Arabis caucasica*			Prune	Prune						
16 *Potentilla alba*										
17 *Arabis caucasica* 'Flore Pleno'				Prune						
18 *Santolina virens*	Prune				Prune					
	INTERIM PLANTING									
Rudbeckia 'Marmalade'		Sow	Sow				Deadhead	Deadhead	Lift	
Verbascum	Plant	Plant				Deadhead	Deadhead		Lift	
Centaurea gymnocarpa	Sow		Plant						Lift	
Dahlia		Plant	Plant	Stake			Deadhead	Deadhead	Lift	
Senecio maritima	Sow		Plant						Lift	
Hibiscus 'Coppertone'	Sow		Plant						Lift	
Ricinus 'Impala'	Sow		Plant	Stake					Lift	
Amaranthus hyponchondriacus (prince's feathers)	Sow	Sow	Sow			Deadhead	Deadhead		Lift	
Amaranthus caudatus	Sow	Sow	Sow			Deadhead	Deadhead		Lift	

THE GARDEN IN WINTER

Far from dreading winter, I look forward to it. The resting garden has an austere beauty that makes a welcome contrast to the colorful and exuberant growth of summer. There are days of dazzling brilliance when the garden is wonderfully still, except for a few foraging birds. These are moments to savor the flowering and foliage plants that are undaunted by cold and rough weather or the shapes and patterns accentuated by the long shadows cast by a low sun. Sometimes snow transforms the garden, the familiar taking on mysterious shapes and forms under the white blanket. The silver-gray shroud of frost is less heavy; but it, too, can change the character of the garden, giving an intriguing outline to stems, leaves and seedheads.

Although it is possible to devote an area of the garden to winter-flowering and evergreen plants, that is not an option I would recommend. My own preference is to rely on the overall design of the garden, with flowering plants and foliage color providing welcome accents and details. At no other season are the structural elements – walls, paved areas, hedges and less formal groupings of shrubs and trees – so important in the garden's design.

Evergreen foliage is invaluable for the way it gives mass and solidity to the garden. This is true whether you allow plants to grow naturally or whether they are trimmed and shaped as hedges or topiary specimens. Even if you confine yourself to the conifers, the color range includes blue-grays and golds as well as every shade of green. Deciduous hedges that hold on to their russet leaves, such as beech and hornbeam, are less dense, but they too look solid in the winter months.

The colors of winter are usually muted, but the flowers are often of exquisite or subtle beauty, and some are deliciously

fragrant. The dwarf bulbs are among the most useful links between autumn and spring. The apparently fragile flowers of crocus species, *Cyclamen coum, Iris reticulata,* scillas and snowdrops (*Galanthus*) – to make a choice selection – stand up remarkably well to rough weather. They look best planted thickly in large groups, but it is worth having a few in pots so that they can be appreciated from close quarters through a window.

Yellow is the color of some of the best winter-flowering shrubs, such as *Corylopsis pauciflora,* mahonias and the witch hazels (*Hamamelis*). But there are whites and pale pinks in the viburnums and the long-flowering *Prunus* x *subhirtella* 'Autumnalis'. The strongest colors among shrubs are provided by the early camellias and rhododendrons and the lime-tolerant *Chaenomeles.*

Yet another range of colors is added by twigs and stems that color well – the white of birches and *Rubus cockburnianus,* the yellow of *Cornus stolonifera* 'Flaviramea' and the red of *C. alba* 'Sibirica' or *Salix alba* 'Britzensis'. These, and long-lasting berries such as the round white drops of *Symphoricarpos,* are more vivid than many winter flowers. Also recommended are the members of the *Sorbus* family that bear white berries, especially *S. cashmiriana.*

Although relatively few herbaceous plants brave the winter months, some are of outstanding merit. It is worth going to some trouble, for example, to build up an attractive collection of bergenias, hellebores and pulmonarias.

Plants of quiet beauty such as the hellebores, or of light but delicious fragrance such as *Chimonanthus praecox,* need to be well placed to be fully appreciated. They are often best sited near a path, or in a spot where they can be seen from a window; or at least near the house.

Page 133: On a misty winter morning the outlines of a collection of conifers are etched and highlighted by frost.

Left: *Crocus tommasinianus* flowers toward the end of winter and can often be found in the snow waiting patiently for a sunny day to open its silver-lilac petals. Like many winter-flowering bulbs, it is happiest left undisturbed where it can propagate itself by seed: but it can also be grown in a pot for a year and then planted out.

Left, below: Rich red berries stand out among tough leathery leaves of a female plant of *Skimmia japonica*. Berries will only be produced if male flowers, on the same or a different plant, are present near by. The all-male cultivar 'Rubella' has panicles of pinky red flower buds that last all winter. Skimmias are small shrubs that like a shady position with fertile, acid soil.

This page, top left: The evergreen, ground-covering leaves of London Pride (*Saxifraga* x *urbium*) make a dense mat that suppresses weeds all year round. Their leathery texture makes them resistant to cold, and they emerge from the frost quite unscathed.

Top right: Hoary hairs of frost outline the tracery of the stalks of *Viburnum opulus* on which some translucent berries still hang. This species has large corymbs of small fertile white flowers surrounded by showy florets in the summer. The leaves turn to deep yellow in autumn as the berries are produced.

Right: Frost and mist have completely enveloped *Corylus avellana* 'Contorta'. The curious habit of its branches earns it the common name of corkscrew hazel. It is slower-growing than the common hazel. The catkins add to its interest.

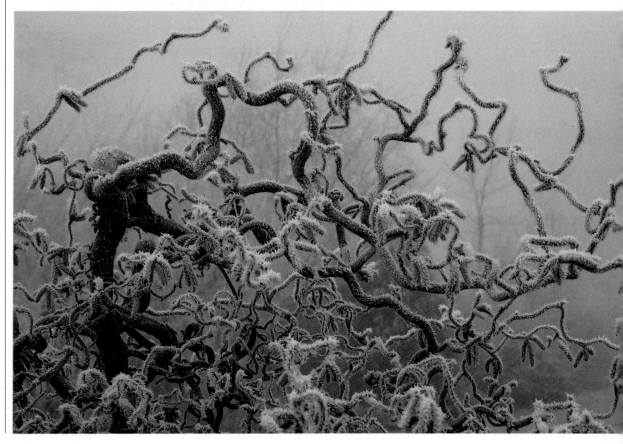

THE MAINTENANCE YEAR

The following section of the book provides a basic calendar of maintenance for all four seasons, covering all the operations that are required in the exemplary all-purpose garden illustrated on the following pages.

I felt it would be useful to relate the maintenance calendar to a specific garden, rather than dealing with the subject in a limbo. In the specimen garden I have devised for this purpose, the spring border receives sun only in the morning, and includes shade-loving plants in a range of blues and yellows. The summer border includes sun-loving herbaceous plants following a fairly strict color composition of silver, white, pink, purple, yellow, orange and red, with shrubs for all-year height and texture and bulbs to extend the season. Spring-flowering *Prunus* × *subhirtella* 'Autumnalis' is shielded from the lawn by shrubs planted in a curve. The vegetable garden is sunny from mid-morning onward with a few fruit bushes in the sunniest position. Wall shrubs and trained fruit trees are planted against the walls to make the most of their warmth.

Alongside the plan on pp. 138-9, the two borders are shown in three separate smaller plans, showing the plants that are predominant in each season.

The All-Seasons Garden: Plan

SPRING BORDER

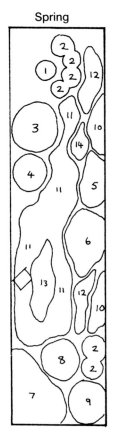

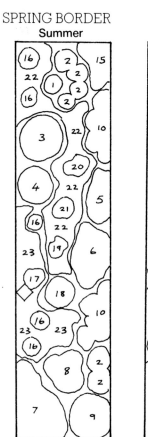

Spring   Summer   Autumn

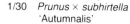

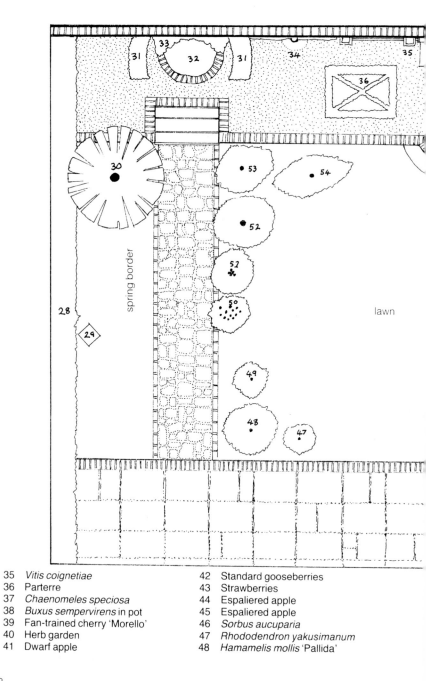

spring border

lawn

1/30	*Prunus* × *subhirtella* 'Autumnalis'	
2	*Heuchera* 'Palace Purple'	
3	*Viburnum* × *bodnantense* 'Dawn'	
4	*Helleborus orientalis*	
5	*Saxifraga* × *urbium*	
6	*Euonymous fortunei* 'Sparkle 'n' Gold'	
7	*Miscanthus caerulea* 'Variegata'	
8	*Helleborus corsicus*	
9	*Iris foetidissima*	
10	*Primula vulgaris*	
11	*Galanthus nivalis*	
12	*Eranthis hyemalis*	
13	*Anemone blanda*	
14	*Hepatica nobilis*	
15	*Cornus canadensis*	
16	*Digitalis* × *mertonensis*	
17	*Acanthus spinosus*	

18	*Doronicum plantagineum*
19	*Filipendula ulmaria* 'Aurea'
20	*Sisyrinchium albidum*
21	*Brunnera macrophylla* 'Dawson's White'
22	*Myosotis*
23	*Narcissi* (mixed)
24	*Hosta* 'Thomas Hogg'
25	*Hosta fortunei* 'Albopicta'
26	*Hosta fortunei aureomarginata*
27	*Hosta tardiana*
28	*Fagus sylvatica* hedge
29	Obelisk
30/1	*Prunus* × *subhirtella* 'Autumnalis'
31	Yew (*Taxus baccata*)
32	Pool
33	Grotto
34	*Rosa* 'New Dawn'

35	*Vitis coignetiae*
36	Parterre
37	*Chaenomeles speciosa*
38	*Buxus sempervirens* in pot
39	Fan-trained cherry 'Morello'
40	Herb garden
41	Dwarf apple

42	Standard gooseberries
43	Strawberries
44	Espaliered apple
45	Espaliered apple
46	*Sorbus aucuparia*
47	*Rhododendron yakusimanum*
48	*Hamamelis mollis* 'Pallida'

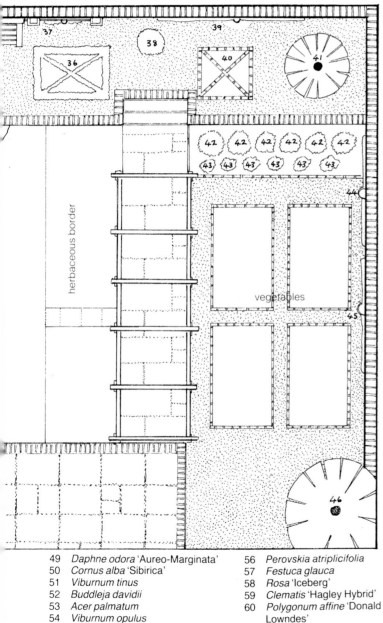

herbaceous border

vegetables

HERBACEOUS BORDER

Spring	Summer	Autumn

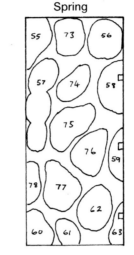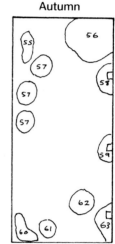

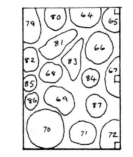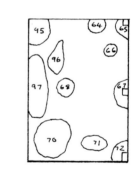

49 *Daphne odora* 'Aureo-Marginata'
50 *Cornus alba* 'Sibirica'
51 *Viburnum tinus*
52 *Buddleja davidii*
53 *Acer palmatum*
54 *Viburnum opulus*
55 *Stachys lanata*
56 *Perovskia atriplicifolia*
57 *Festuca glauca*
58 *Rosa* 'Iceberg'
59 *Clematis* 'Hagley Hybrid'
60 *Polygonum affine* 'Donald Lowndes'
61 *Sedum* 'Autumn Joy'

62 *Weigela florida* 'Variegata'
63 *Clematis* 'Royal Velours'
64 *Rosa glauca*
65 *Rosa* 'Maigold'
66 *Berberis thunbergii atropurpurea*
67 *Clematis* 'Ville de Lyon'
68 *Sedum atropurpureum*
69 *Pulmonaria saccharata*
70 *Iris unguicularis*
71 *Salvia officinalis* 'Purpurascens'
72 *Rosa* 'Danse du Feu'
73 *Chrysanthemum maximum*
74 *Cosmos*
75 *Phlox paniculata*
76 *Anemone japonica*
77 *Monarda didyma*
78 Petunias
79 Heliotrope

80 *Malva moschata*
81 *Rudbeckia fulgida*
82 *Anthemis tinctoria* 'E.C. Buxton'
83 *Achillea* 'Gold Plate'
84 *Dahlia* 'Bishop of Llandaff'
85 *Lychnis arkwrightii*
86 *Begonia semperflorens* (red)
87 *Crocosmia* 'Lucifer'
88 *Tulipa fosteriana* 'Purissima'
89 *Tulipa* 'Arkadia'
90 *Tulipa kaufmanniana* 'Fritz Kreisler'
91 *Tulipa* 'Smiling Queen'
92 *Tulipa* 'Athleet'
93 *Tulipa* 'Henry Ford'
94 *Tulipa* 'Groenland'
95 *Iris danfordiae*
96 *Iris reticulata*
97 *Iris histrioides*

SPRING

SPRING

With warmer weather and steady speeding up of growth, this is a very busy time in the garden. Late frosts can be a major worry, and you should be ready to protect tender new growth.

Over the winter, leaves and twigs will have continued to be blown down and into the garden from the outside. Now is the last chance to clear all these away. Leaves can be composted if there is space; twigs should be burnt, as there is little time to put them through a shredder and compost them at this time of year. Otherwise, bag up debris for disposal with the garbage.

Carefully tread down any ground on and in flowerbeds lifted by frosts.

Before the spring gales take their toll and the vegetation starts into growth, make a final check that all supports are sound.

Pests become active and begin to multiply as the weather warms in late spring. Spray or pick off as soon as they are spotted.

Complete ordering or buying seed as soon as possible.

Borders and beds

Early spring is the last chance to tidy up the borders. Finish cutting back herbaceous perennials. In mild dry weather, complete digging any new areas ready for planting up. All weeds must be removed from between the emerging crowns of perennials and a general fertilizer hoed in before applying a good mulch of pulverized bark or leaf compost.

Sow annuals, starting with hardy ones such as cornflower, mignonette, night-scented stock, rudbeckia, sunflower and sweet peas straight into the ground where they are to flower. Half-hardy ones, such as begonias, impatiens, petunias, tobacco plants and zonal pelargoniums, will need to be germinated in heat and pricked out before you can plant them out. If space is at a premium, it may be better to buy plants from a garden center later on, when the soil begins to heat up. Be patient with the half-hardy ones which will not withstand a late frost. When all risk of frost is past, plant chrysanthemums and dahlias.

Deadheading the bulbs will be a major task throughout the spring, as it is important that all their energies are directed to building up the bulbs for the following year, rather than producing seeds. Remember to make notes of any uneasy color combinations, so that you can move the bulbs when they have finished flowering and the leaves are just dying down. Snowdrops can be moved while still in full leaf.

Seeing bulbs in other gardens may also give you ideas for next year's display, so take photos, perhaps, and find out their names so that you will be ready to order the ones you want from catalogs or buy them in a garden center when you may no longer remember the flower.

A number of autumn-flowering bulbs, many of which are tender, can be planted in late spring, after the last frost; crinum, crocosmia, gladiolus hybrids and species (*G. colvillei and G. callianthus*), tigridia and tritonia.

Trees, shrubs and climbers

Late snowfalls may still cause branches to break under the weight, so brush the accumulated snow off as soon as possible.

When the weather is mild and dry, finish preparing sites for new plantings. Plant deciduous hedges, trees and shrubs, roses and climbers in early spring, while they are still dormant, and evergreen conifers and broad-leaved shrubs and climbers towards the end of spring. When buying stock, look for a good, well-balanced basic framework with plump buds.

Take care when planting to ensure that the hole is large enough to spread out the roots completely and fill in with good compost and some added nutrients. Taller trees should be given a short stake (no more than one-third the height of the trunk) to provide support in the first years, when the plants are becoming established. A mulch of pulverized forest bark of well-rotted leaf mold will help conserve moisture ture through the summer.

Finish tidying up dormant trees and shrubs that you know have old, dead or damaged wood, and cut hard back shrubs such as buddleja, potentilla and spirea that flower on the current year's wood. Other pruning can be carried out during the growing season, when it is easier to see what needs to be cut out; a good time to do this is when you are deadheading.

Hybrid tea and floribunda roses need to be carefully pruned hard back to just above an outward-growing bud. Make sure the cut is slanting away from the bud. Shrub roses and climbers should simply have old wood and weak growth removed.

Large-flowered clematis need pruning back to approximately 2 or 3 feet (60-90cm) from the ground, just above a strong bud.

As spring shrubs, such as *Corylopsis pauciflora*, forsythia, hamamelis and osmathus, finish flowering, prune carefully and shape them at the same time.

During the first half of the season prune shrubs such as *Cornus alba* and *Salix alba* that are grown for their winter display of young colored twigs.

Lawns

This is the time of year when the grass will look its most tired, as it will have made almost no growth during the winter. It is also an important time to carry out major maintenance operations, and before long the lawn will need regular cutting again.

cutting again.

Rake out the thatch of old grass and moss that accumulates over the year. The bare patches revealed by this operation should be repaired by resowing or patching with turf. Weak edges should be consolidated and resown if necessary.

Any waterlogging will be most evident at this time of year, and spiking should relieve this problem, particularly if it is due to compaction. If it is due to bad drainage, it may be worth considering digging a trench to carry surplus water away.

Give the lawn its first cut when it is 2 to 3 inches (6-8cm) high. Do not cut short, but lower the mower blades for successive cuts. Apply a general fertilizer and moss killer, if necessary.

Prepare the site for a new lawn by digging and raking carefully and rolling to make a level site, before sowing. Use a board and work backward to avoid trampling the surface. Sow seed or, for a more instant effect, use turfs purchased from a reliable source.

Pots

Prepare pots for summer-flowering annuals by filling them with a good, well-drained and moisture-retentive potting compost which has enough nutrient to see plants through to the end of the summer. Plant them and water as necessary. Watering will depend on the amount of rainfall but should be approximately once a week in mid-spring, although by the end of the season daily watering may be necessary. Always give the plants a plentiful amount of water, not just a sprinkling.

Pot-grown shrubs will need their annual top dressing incorporating a good slow-release fertilizer.

Fruit, vegetables and herbs

Complete the preparation of beds, raking out ground that you left over the winter to be broken up by frost and working the surface to a fine tilth ready for sowing.

There are many vegetable crops to start from seed throughout the spring, either sown straight into the open ground or raised in a warm place and planted out later.

The earliest of all – lima beans, carrots, peas and parsnips — can be planted straight into the ground; while, if there is space under glass, brassicas, celery, leeks, lettuce, squash and onions can be sown in heat and pricked out. If there is not space, wait until the ground is just warming up and sow in protected seedbeds in the garden. Later, when plants are ready to set out, french and runner beans, beets, spinach, sweet corn and turnips can be planted in the ground. As seedlings develop, they will need thinning and the beds will require weeding.

In early spring, potatoes can be set out in a light airy spot to start into growth. Plant first earlies two to three weeks before the last frosts are expected. Second earlies and then maincrop will follow. When shoots begin to show, earth up the line. Protect tops from unexpectedly late frosts. Onion and shallot sets can also be planted.

Be sure to have finished pruning fruit trees and bushes before growth starts. Any new plantings should likewise be completed and staking carried out where necessary. Apply fertilizers. Spray peach and apricot trees with Bordeaux mixture against leaf curl. Also, spray apples at pink-bud stage with fungicide to control powdery mildew and pesticides to control aphids, apple suckers and capsid bug. Do not delay this operation until trees are in blossom, or you will be in danger of killing beneficial pollinating insects such as bees.

Beds which contain only bushes of soft fruit such as currants, raspberries or gooseberries should be mulched or sprayed with a residual herbicide that will prevent germination of weed seeds throughout the growing season.

New strawberry beds can be planted now and established beds covered with cloches to hasten the crop. Before the flowers appear, put down a mulch of straw or black plastic to prevent weed growth and keep the fruit clean.

As soon as the soil begins to warm up and is dry enough, and the weather mild, sow annual herbs such as chervil, dill and summer savory. Parsley is difficult to germinate; it is sown in early spring and the seed watered with boiling water but warm conditions are most likely to give success. Perennial herbs such as rosemary, thyme, winter savory and lavender can be sown in pots and pricked out ready for planting in the summer.

SUMMER

SUMMER

There are plenty of jobs to keep the keen gardener busy in summer, but later in the season especially there is a chance to relax. However, never let weeds get out of control, and keep an eye open for pests such as greenfly and blackfly or caterpillars, and diseases such as mildew and blight. Spray with pesticides or fungicides as necessary.

Sweep paths regularly to tidy away debris blown about by the wind. Annual weeds and some debris can be composted, but perennial weeds together with prunings and coarse debris that cannot be disposed of in the household garbage should be burned to prevent the spread of both disease and weeds.

Borders and beds
Pull up spring bedding of wallflowers, daisies and forget-me-nots that have finished flowering to make way for the summer display. Prepare the soil, fertilize it and plant out young plants when there seems little further risk of late frost. Later in the season pansies can be planted out for a late-autumn and winter display.

Carefully hoe the borders or pull weeds by hand, making sure you don't disturb roots of herbaceous plants and shrubs. Apply fertilizer in early summer if this was not done in spring.

The display of annuals can be extended into late summer and early autumn by sowing seeds where plants are to flower. Thin seedlings as soon as you can handle them.

Complete any staking of tall herbaceous plants early in the season (see Spring). Deadhead carefully and regularly throughout the summer to encourage plants to bloom for longer. Perennials include campanulas, delphiniums, lupins, peonies and phlox. Annuals include clarkia, cornflower, cosmos, marigolds and sweet peas.

Sow biennials for next spring and summer in a seedbed and thin out seedlings. Summer-flowering biennials such as canterbury bells, hollyhocks and sweet williams that were sown the previous year should be planted out. Sow and thin perennials in a nursery bed for transplanting the following spring.

Cuttings of border pinks can be taken from non-flowering stems and planted into the border in a spot where some sand has been incorporated.

Water the borders regularly if the weather becomes hot and dry.

Continue deadheading the last tulips. To make space for a summer bedding display you may need to move bulbs to a trench in another part of the garden, where they can mature. When the leaves have died down, they can be lifted and stored.

Tulips should not be allowed to dry out immediately after flowering and benefit from an extra feed as they mature. This applies to both species tulips, which should be left *in situ*, and hybrids, which will degenerate if left in the ground and split into numerous bulblets. To save hybrids for next year, lift after the leaves have turned brown, and store in a dry airy spot until early autumn, when they can be planted out again.

Complete planting of tender autumn-flowering bulbs. Anemones de Caen can also be planted for late flowering.

Toward the end of the summer, start to think about next year's spring display of bulbs and order stock soon to avoid disappointment.

Trees, shrubs and climbers
Water all newly planted trees, shrubs and climbers, particularly during periods of drought. It is important that watering is not merely on the surface of the soil, as this would draw roots up, rather than down where reserves can be found. Thorough drenching of the soil every few weeks is more beneficial than a light sprinkling every other day.

Carefully deadhead shrubs, such as buddlejas, kolkwitzia, lilac and philadelphus, and climbers such as *Clematis montana*, shaping the shrub at the same time to ensure that all energies go into making strong new growth. It is important when dealing with rhododendrons and azaleas not to damage the following year's flower bud that forms just below the bud of the current year. Any shrubs such as *Viburnum opulus* and pyracantha that produce berries in the autumn should be left alone.

Prune wisteria by cutting back the long straggly shoots to within 6 inches (15cm) of the main stem.

Deadhead repeat-flowering roses. To ensure a generous second crop of blooms it is advisable to prune the stem to just above the first true leaf (one with seven leaflets, at least).

Start clipping privet and other fast-growing hedges. Toward the end of the summer, trim slower-growing hedges such as those of beech, box, hornbeam and yew.

Lawns
Mow once a week until mid-summer, when growth may require twice-weekly cuts. Keep the grass not less than 2 inches (5cm) high – a little longer in dry conditions. A second application of fertilizer will improve the turf but will mean that mowing will need to be more frequent. To control weeds, treat the whole lawn with a selective herbicide, or better still spot-treat large broadleaved weeds such as plantain, daisies or dandelion.

Regular watering, preferably with a sprinkler, will maintain the grass in a healthy green state.

Pots

Summer is the time when pot-grown plants will need most attention as they require frequent and thorough watering. This means once a day in early summer, rising to twice a day in mid-summer. The amount of water given can be reduced as the days grow shorter.

The best time to water is early morning and late afternoon. When watering make sure that all the compost is wetted. Supplement nutrients in the compost with a water-soluble fertilizer once a week. This treatment will result in a healthy display that brims over the pots with exuberance.

Deadhead flowers of begonias, nicotiana and pelargoniums as they fade, and pick off any blemished leaves.

Plant for autumn display if there is space to keep pots.

Fruit, vegetables and herbs

Plant out hardened seedlings of brassicas, celery and lettuces and water well.

Further sowings of vegetables will ensure an uninterrupted supply of fresh produce through the summer until early autumn. French beans and runner beans, zucchini, pumpkins and squashes, as well as beets, Chinese cabbage and sweet corn (in blocks), can all be sown with success. There is still time, too, for a further sowing of carrots, more lettuce and a quick crop of radishes and turnips. Toward the end of the summer, purple sprouting broccoli, savoy cabbages and winter greens should be planted out for harvesting during the winter months.

Thin seedlings as they come up, and make sure that weeds are not competing with the vegetables, but take care not to damage the crop when pulling weeds. Hoe frequently between the rows; aim to keep the surface of the soil moving to prevent seeds germinating or weeds from putting down roots.

Hill up maincrop potatoes and start to harvest earlies in mid-summer. (It takes about 100 to 110 days for first earlies to mature, 110 to 120 days for second earlies and 125 to 140 days for maincrop potatoes, depending on the weather.)

Start picking vegetables as you need them — beans, cabbages, carrots, cauliflowers, zucchini, lettuces and radishes will all be ready. Remember that they will be most tasty if harvested when they are young and tender. If you have a freezer, carefully blanch and freeze produce in batches.

Alpine strawberries for next summer can be sown in the seedbed now. Young offshoots of old strawberry plants that are going to be required for replanting should be pegged down and any surplus runners cut off.

Protect soft fruit and cherries from birds with a net as soon as the fruit begins to color and check daily that nothing has gotten caught under the net.

Start picking cherries and soft fruit: first will come strawberries and then raspberries; gooseberries and redcurrants will follow later and are easiest to harvest if grown as neat standards.

Vigorous and restricted apple trees (cordons, espaliers and dwarf pyramids) and fan-trained cherry trees will benefit from summer pruning, in which all new growth is shortened to four or five buds, allowing light and air to reach the ripening fruit. When apples have finished flowering, spray against capsid bug, woolly aphid and apple sawfly.

Plant out perennial herbs raised in pots earlier in the year.

AUTUMN

AUTUMN

The colors of dying foliage are among the major delights of autumn, but when at last leaves fall, they must be swept up and cleared away. It can be demoralizing to clear fallen leaves and the next day to find that nearly as many have covered the garden again. It is a question of striking a happy medium between raking every other day for a month and leaving the leaves so long that grass is damaged, and smaller plants suffer, under the soggy cover of vegetation.

Disposing of leaves can be a problem, as the quantity may be too much to cope with on the compost heap. However, it is worth composting as much material as you have space for. A shredder can be used to break down woody materials.

Do as much weeding as possible to clear beds for the winter and to prevent seeding.

Borders and beds

If there is a warm spell at the beginning of the autumn and the summer has been dry, a little watering may be necessary to prevent perennials such as helenium, goldenrod, asters, chrysanthemums and lilies from wilting and to help them complete their cycle in good conditions. Ease off watering as the season advances, as it is best for the plants to be on the dry side to survive the winter.

Continue to deadhead late-flowering herbaceous plants and cut back those that are beginning to look unsightly. More attractive leaves can be left to furnish the border during the winter and help protect perennial crowns during the coldest weather.

Any attractive seed heads can be picked and dried for winter arrangements in the house.

Lift dahlias carefully and place in a box, covered in peat, and store in a dark, frost-free position.

Finish lifting summer bedding to make space for spring displays of bedding or bulbs, and plant out biennials such as daisies, forget-me-nots and wallflowers. Pelargoniums, fuchsias and heliotrope can be potted up, if you have space, and saved for next year. If you do not have a frost-free space, then the pots can be stored outside in a "clamp" – as carrots and potatoes were traditionally kept throughout the winter – covered in a good layer of straw held in place by soil.

Autumn is the best time to lift and split clumps of herbaceous perennials that are becoming too big or are thinning in the center. Discard the old core and replant healthy outer pieces of the crown. New plants can also be put in now and protected with a mulch.

Complete buying bulbs as soon as possible to be sure of quality (stored bulbs deteriorate) and a wide choice. The bulbs available in autumn include spring-flowering ones such as anemones, crocuses, eranthis, fritillaries, bulbous irises, scillas, snowdrops and tulips; but in this season it is also possible to buy some autumn-flowering bulbs such as colchicums, crocuses, snowflakes and sternbergia, and summer-flowering alliums, alstroemerias, species gladiolus, lilies and nomocharis. As soon as they arrive, plant bulbs in their flowering positions, in general to a depth of 4 to 6 inches (10-15cm). However, many bulbs can be planted somewhat deeper, making it possible to grow herbaceous perennials over them, which will then cover the dying leaves of spring flowerers. Deep planting is advisable in cold areas, as it will help bulbs to survive the winter. All bulbs like a well-drained soil, but some like a sun-baked position, others the dappled shade of deciduous trees.

Lift any half-hardy bulbs you wish to save for next year, clean and dry them and store them in a box in a cool, frost-free place.

A generous mulching of spent mushroom compost spread on the border will protect the crowns of plants through the cold winter months, provide plenty of nutrients throughout the growing season, prevent weeds from germinating, and also conserve plenty of moisture in the soil beneath throughout a long period of drought.

Pots

Continue to water pot-grown plants about once a week, less as the season progresses. They should not be allowed to become bone dry but should never be waterlogged.

Before the first frost, bring in any tender plants that have been out for the summer. Put out displays of pansies and late-winter flowering bulbs such as early daffodils, eranthis, small irises and snowdrops. If you have space to keep additional pots, plant later-blooming daffodils, tulips and lilies so that they are ready to move out when they are about to flower to replace pots of faded plants. The aim should be to have something in flower on most days of the year.

Plant up bowls of bulbs that have been specially treated for forcing and store them in a dark, frost-free place for six weeks or until they have formed a good root system. They can then be brought into the light and watered lightly, but keep cool until the shoots have greened up.

Trees, shrubs and climbers

Continue to deadhead roses, as they will continue to flower until the coldest weather sets in, although shyly.

Hedge cutting should be finished early in autumn, and shrubs and climbers should be pruned as they finish flowering. Check all ties and supports for climbers before the autumn gales.

Autumn is a good time for planting. To prepare any areas for new plantings, first remove all perennial weeds, root and all (these weeds are not suitable for composting). Then double-dig the ground, incorporating any organic matter — compost, peat, well-rotted farmyard manure — you are able to acquire, and some slow-release fertilizer.

At the beginning of the season, plant evergreens, such as box, daphnes, rhododendrons, *Viburnum tinus* and yew. Later on, you can start planting deciduous species such as acers, hamamelis, cornus and viburnums. Underplant specimen shrubs with spring-flowering bulbs while they are still young, as it becomes more difficult when the roots begin to spread.

Lawns

Continue cutting grass once a week in early autumn. When there is a marked slowing of growth towards the middle of the season, give the lawn its last trim before winter, setting the mower blades high.

Toward the end of autumn, give the lawn a good rake to clear the leaves, moss and straggly weeds together with any loose clippings that cause a thatch to build up around the base of grass blades.

Vegetables, fruit and herbs

There will still be plenty of harvesting to do in the vegetable garden. Beans and zucchini will continue to crop until the frosts; there will be cabbages (red and white), Chinese cabbage, cauliflowers, late lettuces, squash, pumpkins and sweetcorn. Onions should be dried off ready for the stems to be plaited together before they are hung in a dry position.

Leeks and root crops such as beets, carrots, parsnips and turnips can be pulled as necessary, and maincrop potatoes should be lifted and stored in a well-ventilated, dry and frost-free spot.

As vegetables finish cropping, clear beds and dig over while the weather is still fine, manuring them as you go.

Sow lamb's lettuce, winter lettuce and spinach. Lima beans and round-seeded peas can also be sown for an early crop in the spring.

Plant out spring greens and winter cabbage. Endive plants for forcing can be lifted toward the end of autumn and potted up.

Begin harvesting apples by picking early varieties such as 'Empire', 'Wealthy' and 'Yellow Transparent', which will need eating immediately. Mid-season varieties, such as 'Cortland', 'Grimes Golden' and 'McIntosh', and particularly late varieties such as 'Idared', 'Yellow Delicious' and 'Winesap', together with the cookers 'Greening' and 'Rome Beauty', are more suitable for keeping. They should be picked from the tree before they drop and become damaged. Store them in rows that do not touch, in a frost-free place with a slightly moist atmosphere.

Pears can also be harvested throughout in late autumn.

If the strawberry bed is due for renewal, either transplant young pegged plants once they have rooted or buy new certified stock that will be virus-free.

New rhubarb plants can also be planted in late autumn.

Order fruit trees and bushes and, if you are expecting a delivery before the winter, prepare ground by digging carefully and incorporating organic matter. Ensure that you have erected suitable supports for training espalier apples, raspberries and loganberries.

WINTER

WINTER

Winter is the time to finish tidying the garden in readiness for the spring. It is important to take advantage of any spells of good weather. Finish sweeping and raking up the leaves, if this has not been done, and dispose of those that you are unable to compost. There may be some branches and twigs that drop from overhanging trees; these should also be disposed of.

A few weeds will carry on growing during mild spells, and these should be removed as they appear. Pre-emergence herbicides can be applied to paths to ensure a weed-free season.

Make sure all the garden equipment is clean and in good working order. Sharpen shears and oil all tools to protect them from rust and have them ready for the spring. Garden machinery such as mowers and rotivators should be serviced early in winter to avoid a panic in spring.

If there is space to bring furniture in, give it a good rub down and paint carefully. Make any necessary repairs to outside woodwork.

This will also be your best opportunity of making plans for the future. Seed and plants can be purchased from stores and garden centers or by mail order (catalogs being a valuable source of information); unfortunately, plants sometimes get damaged in the mail and do not always arrive in the best condition. Any new designs for the garden should be worked out and materials ordered.

Borders and beds

Prepare sites for new beds early in winter. Careful double-digging will ensure the best results in the long-term. Incorporate plenty of organic matter, such as garden compost, into the sub-soil and leave the frost to break up the rough clods of top-soil. The beds can be raked out toward the season's end.

Protect early hellebores from the worst weather. Pick *Iris unguicularis* before the birds peck the flowers off.

Toward the end of winter, finish cutting down herbaceous perennials, which by now will be getting very shabby, and spread some compost or a mulch of bark if this was not done in the autumn.

Check stored bulbs and corms, such as gladioli, for rot. Dispose of rotten ones to prevent the spread of disease.

Any lilies that are received or bought in early winter should be planted as soon as conditions are suitable. If they need to be stored for a short period, keep them in a box of moist peat with their "noses" just sticking out. They must be kept plump and healthy until conditions are right to plant them out in late winter or early spring.

Trees, shrubs and climbers

When the weather is good and soil reasonably dry and not frozen, plant roses and deciduous trees (see Spring). Where necessary, provide climbers with a support of trellis or stretched wires. Cut out any dead or damaged shoots. If plants are delivered during very cold weather, keep them in a frost-free place, preferably with some peat around their roots, or heel them in a sheltered spot in the open garden.

Check any existing tree stakes and ties, and secure or renew them if necessary to prevent damage during the winter.

Major pruning of trees can be carried out during the winter and early spring. If you have any large trees that need thinning or taking down, contact a specialized arboriculturist for advice.

Prune wisterias back to a round plump bud. Honeysuckle can also be pruned back in winter. Prune winter-flowering jasmine after it has flowered.

Remove any snow settled on branches with a soft sweeping broom to prevent breakage or damage caused by the weight.

Lawns

In mild conditions, tidy up the lawn by straightening edges and raking off any debris. Never work in very wet or frosty conditions: walking on a frosted lawn can result in brown patches.

Prepare the site for a new lawn thoroughly, making sure you install some drainage if the site is waterlogged. Turf can be laid in good weather, but sowing must wait until the spring.

Pots

Clean and sort any pots ready for planting up in spring.

Check all forced bulbs. Pots of hardy bulbs can be brought indoors just as flowers are about to open. They are best kept in a cool room. Harden off and put outside again after flowering.

Vegetables, fruit and herbs

Clear vegetable beds that have finished cropping and, in good weather, dig over. Leave the ground to be broken by the frost. Lime any areas where you intend to grow brassicas, to help reduce chances of club root disease.

Sow lima beans and peas and cover rows with cloches for soil to warm up sooner.

Finish planting fruit trees and bushes and new strawberries, and plant rhubarb.

Prune apple and pear trees when weather is not too cold. In late winter tie in new raspberry canes and prune out old ones.

SEASONAL PLANT DIRECTORY

TREES

Spring

Aesculus × carnea 'Briottii'
Although more compact and smaller than the common horse chestnut, this tree is only suitable for large gardens as it will reach 25ft (7.6m) in ten years and eventually 40ft (12m). It has upright panicles 10in (25cm) long of deep red flowers that stand out well against the dark green leaves that turn yellow in autumn. It has smooth-coated "conkers". Dislikes a very alkaline soil. **Sun or light shade**

Alnus cordata/Italian alder††
The tall narrowly conical shape of this easy-to-grow tree quickly reaches over 40ft (12 m). The crown is adorned with persistent catkins in the early spring that turn into little round fruit in the autumn. The leaves, somewhat like those of pears, are a shiny dark green on top, lighter beneath. It will grow in any soil, dry or damp, acid or alkaline. **Sun or light shade**

Crataegus laevigata 'Crimson Cloud'*
This hawthorn makes a small rounded tree about 10ft (3m) with glossy green leaves and clusters of large deep red flowers with white patches at the base of each petal. In autumn a plentiful crop of shiny red berries lasts for at least six weeks. **Sun or shade**

Salix caprea 'Weeping Sally'†
This small weeping willow is a female form: displays soft silvery white catkins in spring. Rarely exceeds more than 6ft (1.8m) and forms a graceful umbrella about 5ft (1.5m) wide with branches down to the ground. The leaves are shiny. **Sun or light shade**

Summer

Acer negundo ††
The box elder is a very fast-growing tree reaching nearly 30ft (9m) in ten years. Pinnate leaves have earned it the name of ash-leaved maple. There are variegated forms, of which 'Flamingo' is least vigorous, to 10ft (3m) or a little more; leaves are light pink on opening in spring, maturing to green with white and pinkish markings. **Light shade**

Gleditsia triacanthos 'Sunburst'
The yellow pinnate foliage of this form of the American honey locust recalls that of golden false acacia, *Robinia pseudoacacia* 'Frisia', but this form, unlike the species, is much slower-growing. To 15ft or so (4.5m); needs well-drained soil. Like the species, comes into leaf late, but doesn't bear the same vicious spines. **Sun or light shade**

Metasequoia glyptostroboides*
As a specimen tree this deciduous conifer makes a narrow, very regular pyramid reaching 15ft (4.5m) in 25 years. Trunk is tapered and covered with cinnamon-brown bark. Feathery foliage is bright green in spring, turning yellow in autumn. Prefers a moist position and withstands pollution well. **Sun**

Pyrus salicifolia 'Pendula'/ weeping willow-leafed pear*
This small tree (12ft: 4m) looks spectacular when the long pendulous branches sweep to the ground. The young narrow, willow-like leaves are covered with silky gray down in spring and turn a soft green in summer. Pure white flowers in spring, small inedible pears in autumn. **Sun**

Autumn

Fraxinus oxycarpa 'Raywood'††
Rapidly makes a fine specimen tree reaching some 35ft (10m). Broad canopy looks most striking when it turns a reddy purple in autumn. Leaves attractive all summer. **Sun**

Malus sargentii *†
A small ornamental crab apple tree reaching about 10ft (3m). Cloud of small white scented flowers in late spring. In autumn, bears tiny red fruit. Cultivar 'Rosea' is slightly more vigorous; pale pink flowers. rose in bud. **Sun or light shade**

Parrotia persica*
Spreading habit, with nearly horizontal branches. Reaches 15ft (4.5m) with a spread of about 10ft (3m). Discrete red-stamened flowers appear in late winter against gray flaking bark. In spring leaves unfurl reddish purple and turn dark green. Autumn color of deep yellow, carmine and rusty orange is best in moist, well-drained soil. **Sun**

Sorbus*
A large genus of mostly small to medium trees (15 to 20ft: 4.5-6m) that have year round appeal and are tolerant of dry soils. Whitebeam (*S. aria*) has an upright habit but a rounded crown of large leaves that are bright green above and downy gray beneath. Mountain ash (*S. aucuparia*) has pinnate leaves and the white spring blossom turns to autumn berries in shades of red and orange. In *S. cashmiriana* the fruit is white and, less attractive to birds, stays on the tree until the winter. In areas where borers are a problem the Korean mountain ash (*S. alnifolia*) is to be recommended. **Sun or light shade**

Winter

Acer griseum*††
A tree for all seasons, tolerant of alkaline soil. Grows quickly reaching some 15ft (4.5m). Famed for its beautiful orangey-brown peeling bark. The trifoliate leaves open late, a dark shade of yellow-buff turning dark green in summer and finally deep scarlet and red in autumn. **Sun**

Betula papyrifera††
The smooth white bark of this birch peels off in great sheets revealing glistening new layers beneath. Leaves small, toothed, turning yellow in autumn. Tall open canopy that casts only light shade but reaches nearly 40ft (12m). Any soil. **Sun or shade**

Prunus serrula*
The most important feature of this cherry is its shiny mahogany bark that peels horizontally. A small tree, to 25ft (7.6m) with wide arching branches. The species has willow-like leaves which hide the small white blossoms in spring. Hybrids ('Kanzan' is most famous) are as spectacular as Japanese flowering cherries in spring; they often have coppery young growth and bright autumn color. **Sun or lightest shade**

Prunus × subhirtella 'Autumnalis'*
Small white flowers appear in late autumn, at first thinly, but progressively more, and last through winter, dwindling toward the beginning of spring. Foliage turns yellow and bronze in autumn before falling. Most commonly, single-stem small tree to 12ft (3.6m) but can occur as multi-stemmed shrub. **Sun or light shade**

KEY   ††Fast growers †Slow growers *Plants with more than one season of display   Sizes given are those reached after 10 years unless otherwise specified.

SHRUBS

Spring

Amelanchier canadensis*
A multi-stemmed shrub which can also be grown as a small tree reaching 20ft (6m) or so. Delicate white flowers are followed in early summer by crimson fruit ripening to black. The leaves which unfurl in early spring are a soft copper and turn orange or red in the autumn. Dislikes alkaline soils. **Light shade**

Corylopsis pauciflora
A graceful arching habit characterizes this low-growing shrub; will reach 6ft (1.8m) in height, 5ft (1.5m) in spread. The pale yellow scented bell-shaped flowers open in racemes in early spring before the young pink foliage. The leaves resemble those of hazel. Grow in humus-rich soil. **Light shade**

Cytisus × praecox
The Warminster broom is spectacular for at least two weeks in late spring when the pale yellow blooms cover the cascading twiggy branches. Will reach 4ft (1.2m) and spread to 5ft (1.5m). Foliage is evergreen; new shoots are silky green. **Sun**

Daphne odora 'Aureo-marginata'†
All daphnes have a most powerful scent in early spring but this is perhaps the hardiest and easiest to grow. Rounded habit reaching 4ft (1.2m) high and 5ft (1.5m) wide. Evergreen leaves have pale yellow variegations. Flowers open deep pink and fade to white. **Sun**

Summer

Abelia × grandiflora†
A useful shrub flowering in late summer when little else makes a show. Graceful, with slender, arching branches to 4ft (1.2m) high and as much across. Deciduous in all but the mildest areas. The pale pink, slightly scented flowers stand out against the bright green foliage for several weeks. **Sun**

Buddleja††
Buddlejas will grow in the poorest soil, so they are something of a weed on occasions. They will, however, make a beautiful show for nearly a month in the summer. Buddleja alternifolia has pale mauve flowers in early summer but tends to make a bit of a tangled mess. Cultivars of B. davidii may be pale to deep purple and white and attract quantities of butterflies in late summer. **Sun or light shade**

Kalmia latifolia
An evergreen shrub, which requires the same moist, peaty conditions as rhododendrons. Makes a rounded plant to 6ft (1.8m) with shiny green oval leaves. The five-sided bell-shaped flowers are deep pink in bud, opening much lighter; they last for several weeks. **Sun or light shade**

Kolkwitzia amabilis*
This reliable shrub is covered in bell-shaped pink flowers with a yellow throat in early summer. The plant is vase-shaped, the long stems reaching 6ft (1.8m) or more. Peeling brown bark adds interest in winter. It is much like weigela and deutzia, all three flowering at the same time; kolkwitzia is the hardiest and strongest growing. **Sun**

Autumn

Callicarpa bodinieri*
Much prized for its purple berries which may last several months. Upright habit, with stiff stems a little over 6ft (1.8m). Mauve flowers appear late summer, foliage has a hint of purple in autumn. Add a little peat or leaf mold to poor soils. **Sun or light shade**

Cotoneaster*
There are numerous species, some evergreen, most deciduous, making large, mainly graceful shrubs, such as C. franchetii, or smaller ground-hugging ones, such as C. horizontalis or C. dammeri. White flowers, early summer, are followed by a copious crop of orange to red berries; or, on C. 'Rothschildianus', divaricatus, have good autumn foliage. **Sun or shade**

Euonymus alatus 'Compactus'*†
This cultivar of the common spindle tree is more dense and slower-growing than the species, reaching 4ft (1.2m). Bright pinky autumn color of its foliage is all the more striking if the plant has good drainage. Purplish fruit. Young angled stems that develop corky outgrowths as the plant matures. **Sun or light shade**

Hydrangea quercifolia*†
In ideal conditions the autumn tints of this outstanding hydrangea range from orange through crimson to purple. Oak-like leaves; white flowers in conical panicles from late summer on. In ten years reaches 4ft (1.2m) in height and about 3ft (90cm) in width; never exceeds 6ft (1.8m). **Shade**

Winter

Cornus alba*
The bright red stems of this dogwood are most striking in 'Sibirica'. When pruned biennially in early spring, will reach about 5ft (1.5m). Flowers are white in early summer, and fruit palest blue. Autumn foliage color. The variegated 'Spaethii' (golden) and 'Elegantissima' (silver) have slightly less bright stems but are more attractive in foliage. The species C. stolonifera 'Flaviramea' has yellow stems. Dogwoods thrive in all but the driest soils. **Light shade or shade**

Corylus avellana 'Contorta'†
The twisted branches of this unusual shrub stand out against snow. Yellow catkins in early spring are followed by dark green leaves similar in shape to those of the ordinary hazel, but crinkly. Will eventually make a dense bush to 7ft (2.1m). **Sun or shade**

Hamamelis mollis*
The Chinese witch hazel is a hardy deciduous ornamental that blooms in late winter. Fragrant flowers, with narrow ribbon-like, pale yellow petals, last for nearly a month. Foliage colors well in the autumn. This open, slightly angular shrub reaches 6½ft (2m), 6ft (1.8m) in spread. **Light shade or sun.**

Mahonia aquifolium*
This evergreen shrub has an architectural quality all year round. Leaves are spiny and change from metallic green to bronze-red in the autumn. Fragrant yellow flowers in spring, bunches of blue berries in summer. Will reach 4ft (1.2m) in height and spread. **Shade**

CLIMBERS

Spring

Chaenomeles speciosa*
Grown against a wall, the ornamental quince will reach up to 8ft or more (2.5m). The flowers, which appear in spring, may be white ('Nivalis'), bright rose ('Umbilicata') or dark crimson ('Simonii'). In autumn small, speckled, yellow, apple-like fruit are produced. **Light shade**

Clematis montana††
A vigorous species, will reach 20ft (6m), creating a thick mat of stems that are covered with creamy white, four-petalled blooms in spring. The variety *rubens* and cultivar 'Elizabeth' have pink flowers and are more vigorous still. Some forms have a vanilla-like fragrance. Prune after flowering to prevent rampancy. **Shade**

Cotoneaster horizontalis*
A deciduous shrub for inhospitable dry and shady spots. Stiff branches in a herringbone arrangement will grow close to a wall, reaching 3-4ft (90-120cm). Clothed with pretty pink flowers and round, glossy-green leaves in spring. In autumn, covered with red berries that can last through the winter. Prune only to cut old branches in winter. **Sun or shade**

Lonicera periclymenum 'Early Dutch'/honeysuckle*
Will reach 12-15ft (3.6-4.5m) provided it is planted in deep, moisture-retentive soil which will be most effective if shaded. Stems will twine over a pergola or through another climber, large shrub or tree toward the light where highly scented, creamy colored flowers bloom from spring into summer. **Sun**

Summer

Clematis large-flowered hybrids
There are many large-flowered clematis hybrids that flower from early summer through to autumn, including white 'Marie Boisselot', carmine 'Ville de Lyon' and blue 'Perle d'Azur'. They are best suited to climbing through a host plant, which will provide shade for their roots. They like deep loam that retains moisture. Prune in early spring. **Light shade**

Hydrangea petiolaris*
Also classified as *H. anomala petiolaris*. Slow to establish but will grow to great heights, reaching 50ft (15m), clinging by small aerial roots. Wide flat clusters of white sterile flowers surrounding small, dirty-white, fertile flowers appear in early summer, covering the plant. The peeling, rust-colored bark is appealing in winter. Prune only to guide and restrict vigor. **Shade**

Lathyrus odoratus/sweet pea††
The annual sweet pea requires a rich soil to grow vigorously and attain 6ft or more (1.8m). Blooming will be increased if the highly scented flowers are picked frequently. Seed is available in mixed or single colors (from pure white to deepest purple). **Sun**

Wisteria sinensis††
Well pruned and trained, this vigorous climber will make a beautiful spectacle all year round. Given space, warmth and well-drained soil, will grow to 30ft (9m). Chief glory is long racemes of purple or white flowers that can cover a plant in summer. Delicate, pale green foliage follows. Gray twining stems in winter. **Sun**

Autumn

Clematis tangutica
A late-flowering species with slender stems that will extend to 10ft (3m). The delicate foliage has a gray-blue tint that contrasts well with the nodding, four-petalled, deep yellow flowers. The silky seed tassels begin to appear before last flowers have finished opening. **Light shade**

Parthenocissus tricuspidata††
Excellent self-clinging climber, will grow well almost anywhere. Being very vigorous, needs lots of space and may become rampant in a hot summer. You may need to restrict the roots and prune severely in summer. The deciduous leaves, broadly lobed with toothed edges, turn bright crimson in autumn. The dark blue berries are rarely seen in cold climates. **Sun or shade**

Passiflora caerulea*
The passionflower is rampant in a climate with mild winters and long, hot and humid summers. In less favorable climates, will grow to 12ft (3.5m) and may be damaged by frost. The palmate leaves are evergreen in frost-free conditions. The unusual purple and white flowers appear in summer; followed by yellow egg-shaped fruit. **Sun**

Vitis vinifera 'Purpurea'††
The Teinturier grape is only marginally less vigorous than the species, reaching 8ft (2.4m) in one season. Often best to restrict it to this height by cutting back long shoots in summer and by pruning in winter just above a pair of plump buds. The young white leaves turn pale claret-red and slowly darken to purple in the autumn. **Sun**

Winter

Euonymus fortunei radicans
A very hardy evergreen, which clings by aerial roots and reaches 12ft (3.5m) or more depending on the form. Like ivy, has a juvenile phase in which it produces small, oval, loosely-toothed leaves. Once it stops climbing, it bears larger leaves as well as flowers and fruit. 'Colorata' has leaves that turn reddish-purple in winter. **Shade**

Hedera helix/English ivy††
Ivies give evergreen cover both for walls and on the ground. Will spread to 15ft (4.5m) and climb higher. They prefer alkaline soil. In juvenile phase, have typically lobed-leaves; in the adult forms (climbing ivies only) the leaves are more rounded and the plant bears clusters of yellow flowers followed by black fruit. Numerous cultivars with different shaped and variegated leaves. **Shade**

Jasminum nudiflorum†
Winter jasmine has a weeping habit, so needs careful training to attain its potential spread of 10-15ft (3-4.5m). Pale yellow, small, trumpet-shaped flowers grace the green leafless stems. Avoid a wall that is exposed to the morning sun, as frosted blooms will scorch. **Shade**

Pyracantha coccinea 'Mojave'*
Evergreen except in the coldest climates. Has a stiff upright habit that can be trained effectively against a wall to 12ft (3.5m) or more. The small, dark green leaves have a leathery texture; they are nearly obscured by a froth of small white flowers in early summer. Abundant orange berries persist well into winter. **Shade**

HEDGES

Spring

Cornus mas/cornelian cherry*
Blooms early in the year and grows 6ft (1.8m) in ten years. The small pale yellow flowers appear before the leaves. In a warm climate, small cherry-like fruit appear in autumn. Best pruned early summer. Plant at 2-3ft (60-90cm) intervals. **Sun or lightest shade.**

Crataegus monogyna/hawthorn††
This deciduous hedging plant will make a tight 8ft (2.4m) screen in less than ten years. Covered with a multitude of small white fragrant flowers in mid to late spring, followed by pale green leaves. Best pruned in summer, but if you want to see the autumn berries can be pruned every other year. Plant at 1ft (30cm) intervals. **Sun or light shade.**

Rhododendron yakusimanum†
Makes a low evergreen rounded screen barely 3ft (90cm) tall and wide. The narrow oblong leaves are dark green above, velvety brown below. Bears flowers that are pink in bud, turning white; recently bred hybrids that are slightly more vigorous vary in color from white to scarlet. Requires acid, moisture-retentive soil. Plant every 18in (45cm). **Shade**

Thuja occidentalis
The American arborvitae is a very hardy species; tolerates cold and wet soils. 7ft (2.4m). Evergreen foliage is bright green in spring, turns duller through the season. The western red cedar, *T. plicata*, is less hardy but faster growing, reaching 10ft (3m) if protected from frost and drought early on. Trim both late summer. **Sun**

Summer

Carpinus betulus/hornbeam*
A deciduous tree that responds well to frequent pruning. It will make a dense 8ft (2.4m) hedge in ten years. Leaves turn brown in autumn and subsist well into winter, especially if hedge is clipped late in the season. Grows well in most soils. Plant every 12-18in (30-45cm). **Sun or shade.**

Ligustrum ovalifolium 'Aureum'††
Golden privet. Fast-growing, may require two to three cuts in the season. The golden form is slightly slower, making an 8ft (2.4m) hedge in 6-8 years. Prune early spring, perhaps again early summer. For colder areas the green *L. amurense* or *L. vulgaris* 'Cheyenne' and the golden *L. vulgaris* 'Aureum' are hardier. Plant at 2ft (60cm) intervals. **Sun or light shade.**

Taxus baccata/yew*
Classic English evergreen hedging plant, tight dark green. 7ft (2m) in 10-12 years. Well adapted to grow in most conditions except the coldest. Hybrid species *T. media* is hardier, best represented in cultivation by 'Hicksii'. Trim mid-to-late summer. Plant at 18-24in (45-60cm) intervals. **Sun or shade.**

Viburnum opulus/guelder rose
Vigorous shrub, 8ft (2.5m). Fertile corymbs amid white florets; berries in early autumn. 'Sterile': inflorescence of infertile florets, no berries. 'Compactum': neater, less vigorous form, doesn't require winter pruning necessary to contain the species. 'Aureum' has golden leaves all year. 'Fructo-luteo' and 'Xanthocarpum' have yellow fruit. Plant every 4ft (1.2m). **Sun.**

Autumn

Acer campestre/field maple††
Rugged species. Quickly grows to 10ft (3m) or more. Deciduous leaves typical of the genus turn to shades of red or yellow. Prune winter or summer; summer best to curb growth. Plant at 18in (45cm) intervals. **Sun or light shade.**

Arbutus unedo/strawberry tree†
Grows only in a sheltered garden or mild climate; will not endure severe winters. Slow grower, reaching 5-6ft (1.5-1.8m) in ten years, but in time would make a tree. Large evergreen narrow oval dark green leaves; cream flowers appear late autumn with strawberry-shaped pink fruit. Plant every 3-4ft (90-120cm). **Sun.**

Elaeagnus × *ebbingei*††
An excellent screen in under ten years, reaching 10ft (3m), spreading more than 6ft (1.8m). Evergreen; not absolutely hardy. Large leathery green leaves. Mature plants bear small white fragrant flowers in autumn on the old wood. Best pruned in late summer. Plant at 3ft (90cm) intervals. **Sun or light shade.**

Fagus sylvatica/beech*
Unlike the similar hornbeam, does not tolerate damp soils and cold conditions. Grows best on a well-drained (sandy or chalky) soil. More susceptible to late spring frosts so less likely to achieve 8ft (2.4m) in ten years. Deciduous leaves larger and smoother than hornbeam; remain on the hedge throughout the winter, especially if pruned late in the season. Copper beech a good alternative. Plant every 18in (45cm). **Sun or light shade.**

Winter

Buxus sempervirens/box*
Small round-leaved evergreen shrub, grows slowly, reaches barely 4ft (1.2m) in ten years. Ideal as topiary, stands severe pruning. Variety 'Suffruticosa' has smaller leaves and is good for edging. Box copes with most soils if climate is not too hard. **Sun or shade.**

Camellia
Sheltered garden or mild climate. Evergreen, highlighted in winter or early spring by blooms. *Williamsii* hybrids are among the best and hardiest, reaching 10ft (3m). Abundant flowers, vary in color from white ('Francis Hanger') to pale pink ('J. C. Williams') to darker pink ('Donation'). **Light shade.**

× *Cupressocyparis*
leylandii/Leyland cypress††
If clipped early in growth, makes a first-class screen very fast, at least 15ft (4.5m) in ten years. Gray-green foliage, should be trimmed in late spring and late summer, particularly at first. 'Castlewellan' is golden form. Plant 2½ft (75cm) apart. **Sun or light shade.**

Ilex/holly†
Mostly evergreen hedges. The English holly, *I. aquifolium*, is slow, barely reaching 5ft (1.5m) in ten years; the American holly, *I. opaca*, reaches 7-8ft (2.1-2.4m) in long, hot and humid summers. Species vary greatly in hardiness; most cold-resistant are the blue hollies, *I.* × *merserveae*, and the deciduous *I. verticillata*. Shiny green leaves more or less spiny, with many different kinds of variegation. Female forms need a male pollinator to produce berries. **Sun or shade.**

ROSES

Climbers

Summer

'Gloire de Dijon'*††
From mid-summer on this cultivar is almost continually in bloom. The double, quartered flowers have a soft apricot color with some petals darker and some lighter. The fragrance can be very strong in hot, still weather but rather elusive otherwise. A vigorous climber, will reach 15ft (4.5m), the lower 6ft (1.8m) often remaining bare. **Sun**

'Handel'††
One of the most popular climbing roses, will reach some 20ft (6m) in a hot summer but just over half that in a cooler one. Glossy dark green foliage, needs spraying against blackspot. Flowers beautifully shaped with creamy petals edged in pink. The pink tends to fade as the flowers age. **Sun**

'Madame Grégoire Staechelin'*††
A very vigorous grower reaching up to 20ft (6m). Happy even on a shady wall. Healthy glossy mid-green leaves. Profusion of pink flowers (darker in bud, lighter and with a hint of yellow at the base as they age) early in the season. Hips appearing late summer turn light orange. **Sun or shade**

'New Dawn'*††
A hardy rose, resistant to most diseases, suitable for shady walls, pergolas and fences. Has vigorous lateral habit, growth can exceed 15ft (4.5m) on a wall. Leaves are a shiny light green. Medium-sized flowers are apple-blossom pink with a deeper center, profuse in early summer when they fill the air with a strong fragrance. Second flush in late summer. **Sun or light shade**

Autumn

'Climbing Iceberg'*
A sport of the famous 'Iceberg' shrub, will reach 12ft (3.6m) climbing against a wall. A profusion of clear white flowers carried in trusses down the stems early in the season. On mature plants repeat blossoms continue into the autumn. The pale green foliage is prone to mild attacks of mildew and black spot. **Sun or light shade**

Rosa filipes **'Kiftsgate'*††**
Small orange hips. One of the most vigorous rambling roses, may eventually spread some 50ft (15m). Looks its most spectacular in mid-summer when sweetly scented, creamy white blossoms cascade over gray-green foliage. **Sun**

'Maigold'*
A versatile shrub rose that will also grow as a pillar and can achieve 15ft (4.5m) on a wall. Thick, well-veined leaves, very thorny. From late spring for 6 weeks red-streaked buds are followed by deep yellow flowers which spread their honey-like fragrance around. If deadheaded immediately after flowering, will produce a second flush of flowers in late summer; if not, a crop of hips follows. **Sun**

'Parkdirektor Riggers'*
One of the most colorful of climbing roses, reaches 15ft (4.5m) or more. It has dark green leaves and clusters of deep red flowers that appear first in mid-summer and again in early autumn in nearly equal quantities. **Sun**

Shrub and floribunda

Summer

'Allgold'*
This floribunda has a neat habit, growing to 2ft (60cm) or a little more. Dark, glossy green foliage, which is disease-resistant. The semi-double flowers are a deep golden yellow that never fades, even in hot sunshine, and are unblemished by rain. Starts to bloom early in the season, long-lasting. **Sun**

'Grüss an Aachen'*
This old favorite, of hybrid tea parentage, is sometimes classified as a floribunda and sometimes as an "English rose". Graceful growth to just 3ft (90cm) with pale green leaves. Large scented flowers are freely produced throughout the season (even in shade) are pink in bud, opening pearly-pink and fading to white. **Sun or light shade**

'Madame Hardy'
A vigorous damask rose about 6ft (1.8m) tall with clear green foliage. The beautiful double flowers have a green eye in the center of the pure white petals. The delicious, fresh fragrance fills the air in early summer with a hint of lemon. **Sun**

'Madame Isaac Pereire'*
An old-fashioned bourbon shrub rose with shocking pink large double blooms, beautiful both in bud and fully open. Has a heady scent, particularly during its long mid-summer flowering season. There are a few later blooms in autumn. In a rich soil will quickly reach a height of 6ft (1.8m). **Sun**

Autumn

Rosa glauca*
A tall graceful shrub to 7ft (2.1m) grown chiefly for its light blue-gray foliage. The early-summer display of single white centred pink flowers is followed by a crop of deep red hips. **Sun or light shade**

Rosa moyesii **'Geranium'***
A very erect, tall shrub rose, can reach up to 8ft (2.4m); also suitable for growing up a pillar or high wall. Elongated orange hips in autumn. Single brilliant red flowers with orangey yellow stamens make a striking display in early summer. The leaves are made up of many tiny leaflets. **Sun**

Rosa rugosa **'Alba'***
One of the most rugged of roses, with stout stems to 5ft (1.5m). Makes a dense shrub, attractive in early summer when in flower and in autumn when covered in hips and the leaves turn yellow. The flowers of the species are deep pink but 'Alba' has single, pure white flowers with yellow stamens. All are very fragrant. The hips are bright red, 1in (2.5cm) round, flattened at the top. Other good cultivars include the clear pink 'Frü Dagmar Hastrup' and 'Roseraie de l'Haÿ', double crimson but no hips. **Sun**

Rosa virginiana*
A tall bush, to 6 ft (1.8m), with fierce thorns at the base of the leaf, which is bronzy when young, bright green in summer and turns a vibrant shade of orange in the autumn, complementing the bright red, round hips. The solitary, single flowers are clear pink and slightly scented throughout mid-summer, but not very profuse. **Sun**

PERENNIALS

Spring

Brunnera macrophylla†*
Reminiscent of forget-me-nots. Small vivid blue flowers, in late spring, on stems 1ft (30cm) or taller, rise above large mid-green heart-shaped leaves which may spread to 2ft (60cm). They make rounded mounds that spread to 18in (45cm). There is a variegated form, 'Dawson's White'. **Sun or shade**

Euphorbia††*
E. polychroma is a striking species 18in (45cm) high with sulphur-yellow flower heads in spring held above fresh green leaves which spread to 18in (45cm). E. characias wulfenii stands nearly 3ft (90cm) high and wide. Glaucous foliage, yellowish green flowers. E. griffithii has deep orange flower heads at 2ft (60cm) (spread 2ft/60cm). **Sun or light shade**

Omphalodes cappadocica
Low-growing for ground cover, non-invasive. Does well in deep soil in light shade – for example, under shrubs. Makes thick clumps of hairy heart-shaped leaves with deep veins to 4in (10cm) long. The clear blue flowers stand out above the leaves in early spring. Spreads 1ft (30cm). **Shade or partial sun**

Pulmonaria saccharata/Bethlehem sage
Larger leaves and flowers than common lungwort (P. vulgaris), which is also known as soldiers and sailors or Joseph and Mary for its pink and blue flowers. Both are good ground-cover plants, smothering weeds with their spotted leaves, and flower early in the year. Spread 2ft (60cm). **Shade or partial sun**

Summer

Artemisia 'Powis Castle'††
This hybrid (probably between A. absinthium and A. arborescens) is one of the best gray-leaved perennials. Makes a bushy mound 2-3ft (60-90cm) high, a little more wide. Rarely flowers. Strikes easily from cuttings taken in late summer, and in this way can be overwintered in the coldest areas. **Sun**

Crambe cordifolia†
A stately plant. Bears huge panicles of tiny white flowers on 5-7ft (1.5-2m) stems in early summer. Heart-shaped leaves can be up to 2ft (60cm) long, are usually hairy and deeply veined, spreading to 4ft (1.2m). Usually needs spraying or caterpillars will reduce leaves to a skeleton. Needs deep but very well drained, slightly alkaline soil. **Sun**

Geranium macrorrhizum††*
A semi-evergreen ground-covering perennial. Slightly aromatic leaves are pale green at first; good russety autumn colors. The soft pink flowers are plentiful and long-lasting. Spreads 2ft (60cm). Tolerant of most reasonably deep and well-draining soils. Propagate by division autumn or early spring. **Sun or light shade**

Hosta/plantain lily
Ground-covering. There are numerous species and cultivars with lanceolate or broad leaves that vary in color from deep blue-green to palest yellow or with gold and silver variegations. Purple, mauve or white flowers are generally insignificant, although a few are scented. Main enemies are slugs and snails. Need moisture-retentive soil. **Sun or shade**

Autumn

Aconitum 'Bressingham Spire'
Three ft (90cm) tall, with erect panicles of helmet-shaped deep purple-blue flowers in late summer and autumn. Spreads 18in (45cm). Easy to grow in rich, cool, moisture-retentive soil which will be improved by a mulch in the spring. Do not divide more than every 3-4 years as roots resent disturbance. **Sun or light shade**

Aster × frikartii 'Mönch'
One of the best autumn-flowering perennials, lasts from late summer to mid- or late autumn. Large scented, clear bluish-mauve daisy flowers with yellow centers, on stems nearly 3ft (90cm) tall. Spreads 15in (40cm). For different colors, look for one of the numerous hybrids of A. novi-belgii or the larger A. novae-angliae. **Sun or light shade**

Cimicifuga racemosa†
Superb garden plant. Pure white "bottle-brush" inflorescences up to 1ft (30cm) long on slender, branched stems sometimes reaching 7ft (2.1m) tall. Large divided leaves are attractive all summer, making a mound 4ft (1.2m) across. **Sun or light shade**

Sedum 'Autumn Joy'††*
Attractive all through the year. The young growth of fleshy gray-green leaves appears in spring, followed in summer by large flat heads in matching color; these then turn pink and finally, in autumn, coppery red. The dried seed heads will subsist well into the winter. Grows 2ft (60cm) tall by 2ft (60cm) wide. **Sun or light shade**

Winter

Bergenia cordifolia††*
Evergreen ground-covering plant, large leathery, rounded, glossy green leaves. Each plant will spread to 2ft (60cm). Generous heads of lilac-pink flowers are borne on 18in (45cm) stalks in late winter or early spring. 'Purpurea' has striking foliage that tends to be purplish in winter, and the flowers are darker on red stems. **Sun or light shade**

Helleborus niger/Christmas rose†
Bold, rich, creamy-white flowers with yellow stamens held 1ft (30cm) high above dark green, leathery leaves. Most successful in shade in moist soil which never dries out and where there is protection from wind and rain, which tend to spoil the flowers. Each plant will spread to 18in (45cm). **Shade or light shade**

Heuchera 'Palace Purple'*
An evergreen foliage plant, attractive reddy-purple above, brighter red beneath, heart-shaped, deeply veined leaves that look best in association with grays and pale green. In early summer a delicate spray of minute bell-shaped flowers is produced. **Light shade**

Iris foetidissima/Gladwyn iris*
A hardy iris, will thrive in both dry, inhospitable and more fertile, moist soils. Tall dark green leaves and discreet browny purple flowers which are followed by showy orange seed pods in autumn and winter. 'Variegata' has creamy variegated leaves but rarely flowers so does not produce any seed pods. **Shade**

ANNUALS AND BIENNIALS

Spring

Bellis perennis/daisy
The little pompom flowers of the double cultivated daisy are ideal for carpet bedding, edging or for filling in gaps at the front of the border. They flower from mid-spring on, displaying bright pink, rosy red, crimson and white blossom for several weeks. Sow early summer and plant out in their flowering position in early autumn. **Sun**

Cheiranthus cheiri/wallflower
A scented biennial in shades of yellow, orange, red; flowers for most of second half of spring. Many plants sold are in mixed colors: it is worth growing your own from single colored packs. There are dwarf types (10-12in/25-30cm) and taller ones (15-18in/40-45cm). Sow early summer for flowering the following spring. **Sun or light shade**

Iberis amara/candytuft*
Perhaps one of the easiest annuals to raise, can be sown in late summer for an early display the following spring, or in spring for a summer display. Compact plants 9 to 12in (22-30cm) high with pure white, cream, maroon, carmine, pink, lilac or purple flowers. Seed heads dry well for arrangements. **Sun**

Myosotis/forget-me-not
A useful annual that self-seeds, filling gaps in the spring display of bulbs or among perennials. Color range from rose pink through pale blue to deep indigo blue. Look for the most compact strains, which look less untidy. They should be sown in summer, preferably where they are to flower the next spring, as they are not easy to transplant. **Sun or light shade**

Summer

Angelica archangelica
Stately biennial. If left to seed itself, becomes a bit of a weed; however, the seedlings are easy enough to pull up. The large, deeply divided, bright green leaves are produced the first year. In the second year the thick central stem grows to 10ft (3m) and produces an enormous umbel of greeny white flowers. The leaves can be encouraged to increase in size by cutting off the flower heads as they appear. **Sun**

Centaurea cyanus/cornflower*
Cornflowers are among the hardy annuals that will sow themselves year after year. The blue strains look attractive with the bronze and yellow pot marigold. Other strains come in white and pink. Can be coaxed into flower for late spring if sown in early autumn and overwintered in a cold frame; provided deadheading is thorough, will continue until late summer. **Sun**

Dianthus barbatus/sweet william
Related to carnations, sweet williams have fragrant purple, red or white flowers often with a pale eye or margins. The taller strains are useful for a border, while more compact ones are suitable for bedding out. Usually grown as a biennial – sow in summer and plant out in early spring. **Sun**

Helianthus/sunflower
In 2-3 months will grow from seed to a monster 8ft (2.5m) tall (or more) with a thick stem and wide heart-shaped leaves up to 18in (45cm) long. The bright yellow flowers (up to 1ft/30cm wide) turn to the sun according to the time of day. Will make an immediate impact. **Sun**

Impatiens
In recent years, low compact strains of impatiens have been bred for hardiness, and greenhouses are no longer an essential requirement. Color range includes clear orange, white, pink, salmon and purple. Will brighten up a shady spot all summer. Sow in gentle heat in spring, plant out immediately after last frost. **Shade**

Nicotiana alata/tobacco plant
This is the South American wild species, with the best scent, particularly strong in the evening. Creamy white flowers on 4ft (1.2m) stems. Dwarf strains (to 18in/45cm) most commonly available in shades of white, red, crimson, pink, lime green, purple, picotee and rose pink. Some have a white eye. **Light shade**

Rudbeckia/coneflower, black-eyed Susan
The rich colors of this hardy annual start to light up the garden in late summer but last well into the autumn. There are several different cultivars, the most popular being 'Goldilocks' and 'Marmalade'. The central disk characteristic of the daisy family forms a prominent cone. The tallest (to 2½-3ft/75-90cm) tetraploid hybrids, with single flowers up to 7in (18cm) across, are known as gloriosa daisies. **Sun**

Autumn

Callistephus chinensis/annual or China aster
Asters vary from tall strains for the border or cutting to compact dwarf bedders that can also be grown in pots for late color. Colors include scarlet, white, pink and blue. Flowers can be double, almost pompom-like, or single, the latter like the old-fashioned cottage garden asters. Some have been selected for their resistance to aster wilt, which can ruin a display and persists in the soil a long time. **Sun**

Rhodochiton atrosanguineum
This tender perennial from Mexico can be easily raised from seed and treated as a half-hardy annual sown in heat in spring and planted out as soon as frosts have passed. Rapidly climbs 6-8ft (1.8-2.4m). Deep maroon flowers hanging from inside a carmine calyx. In a hot climate will start to flower before end of summer. Can also be raised from cuttings taken in summer. **Shade or light shade**

Viola × wittrockiana/pansies
There are strains of pansies for every season, but the most precious are those that start to flower in the open in late autumn and last into the winter. Look out for Multiflora, Floral Dance, or Universal series which must be sown in early summer and planted out in their flowering position in late summer or early autumn. Colors include blue, purple, yellow, white, orange, red with some selfs, some bicolors and some blotched or whiskered. **Sun**

BULBS

Spring

Fritillaria imperialis/crown imperial
Opens orange or yellow nodding bell-shaped flowers from mid-spring onward. Can reach 30in (75-80cm). Needs a good well-drained soil. **Sun or light shade**

Muscari armeniacum/grape hyacinth
Spikes of small, bell-shaped, blue flowers with a white rim characterize this mid-spring species that looks good naturalized in grass, growing under shrubs or with late daffodils and tulips. Rarely higher than 9in (22cm). Increases rapidly in well-drained soils. **Sun or lightest shade**

Narcissus species and cultivars/ daffodils
Earliest are some of the dwarf *cyclamineus* cultivars with gently swept-back petals, followed by the large-flowered cultivars and *triandrus* division with slightly drooping flowers. Last, just as the trees break into leaf, come the pheasant's eye narcissi (*N. poeticus*). By careful choice of species and cultivars you can have daffodils flowering throughout the spring. **Sun or light shade**

Tulipa spp. and cultivars/tulips
Tulips start to flower in the middle of the season. Colors vary from pure white to darkest purple, with yellows, pinks, reds and oranges, some spotted, streaked or suffused with contrasting or complementary colors. Most cultivars can be lifted as soon as leaves die down and stored in a dry place. Species and hybrids can be left in ground to flower year after year. **Sun**

Summer

Allium giganteum
One of the tallest onion species, will grow to 4ft (1.2m). Has large rounded heads of densely packed lilac-pink flowers. The leaves, gray-blue, will be damaged by a late frost, so you should plant in well-drained soil in a sheltered site. **Sun**

Arisarum proboscideum/mouse plant
This unusual plant is easy to grow provided it has cool humus-rich soil that never dries out. Glossy arrow-shaped leaves hide small brown flowers with a long mouse-like tail. Grown from bulbs, they also spread by underground rhizomes and quickly make a large patch. **Shade**

Gladiolus callianthus (*Acidanthera murielae*)
Perhaps the only late-summer-flowering scented bulbous species. Each bulb makes a slender plant about 2½ft (75cm) tall with spikes of white flowers that have a dark maroon centre. In cold areas should either be treated as an annual, or lifted after flowering and stored until spring in a frost-free, dry, well-ventilated spot. **Sun**

Lilium/lilies
Many lilies will grow only in acid conditions, but the following are just two of a number of lime-tolerant lilies. The Madonna lily, *L. candidum*, is about 3ft (90cm) tall and has pure white, highly scented flowers. It needs a sunny position; plant shallowly. The Turk's cap lily, *L. martagon*, also reaches 3ft (90cm) but has purple flowers with reflexed petals and needs some shade. **Sun or shade**

Autumn

Colchicum speciosum/autumn crocus
Good for naturalizing in grass where other spring-flowering bulbs are growing: the 12in-high (30cm) leaves appear in spring. The large flowers are pinkish with a white throat, little more than 8in (20cm) high. The white form *album* is equally easy to grow in any well drained soil. **Sun or light shade**

Cyclamen hederifolium*
Native of the Mediterranean. The delicate pale purple flowers appear in early autumn and continue to flower for a month or so. There is also a white form, 'Album'. The silver marbled leaves appear after the flowers fade and last as ground cover through the winter. **Sun or shade**

Dahlia
In small quantities dahlias will make a bright splash of yellow, bronze, orange, mauve and red from late summer right up to the first frost, provided they are regularly dead headed. Easiest to grow are the dwarf varieties raised from seed sown in spring. Recommended is the red-flowered 'Bishop of Llandaff' which needs to be propagated vegetatively but is worth growing for its striking purple foliage. **Sun or light shade**

Nerine
The drier and poorer the soil, the better this South African species will flower. Exotic-looking bluish-pink flowers appear over short strap-shaped leaves on bare stalks in autumn and last until first frosts. In mild climates will need protection (a wall may be sufficient) in winter. **Sun**

Winter

Crocus chrysanthus
A small-flowered yellow species which has many cultivars, some with bronze or purple markings. They bloom in late winter and into spring, well before the large Dutch crocuses. **Sun**

*Eranthis hyemalis/*winter aconites
This hardiest of little plants has been known to bloom under a sheet of ice! Bright yellow flowers surrounded by narrow green leaves appear in mid-winter and last for several weeks, those in the lightest position opening first. More pretty leaves follow. **Shade**

Galanthus/snowdrops
Snowdrops start flowering in mid-winter and last until spring. Most common is *G. nivalis* but there are many other species that vary in size and, on close examination, in the green flower markings. They look best under trees and shrubs and with winter aconites. **Light and shade**

Iris
Iris histrioides 'Major' and *I. reticulata* both have clear blue flowers, the former in late winter, the latter, which is scented, a little later. *Iris danfordiae* is a rich yellow. All three need well-drained soil and plenty of sunshine for their bulbs to ripen in the summer. **Sun**

GLOSSARY

Terms in CAPITAL LETTERS cross-refer to other glossary entries.

Annual A plant whose lifespan — from seed to flowering and death — is less than one year.

Anther The pollen-bearing part of the stamen, usually with two lobes, each containing two pollen sacks.

Axil bud The bud that is found in the angle formed by the junction of leaf and stem.

Bedding plant A plant that is grown and displayed for one season only — as opposed to a border plant, which is permanent. Bedding plants may be ANNUALS, BIENNIALS or TENDER PERENNIALS.

Biennial A plant that requires two growing seasons to complete its life cycle; for example, the foxglove. Leaves are formed during the first year and flowers and seeds the following year.

Bordeaux mixture A fungicide, based on copper sulfate, often used to control potato and tomato blight, scab on apples and pears, and peach leaf curl. It was first used against downy mildew in vineyards in the Bordeaux region of France.

Bulb A modified shoot consisting of a basal fleshy stem or plate that develops roots below and has closely folded-over leaves above: these contain reserve food and protect the flower bud.

Calyx The outer layer of floral leaves. They are normally green but occasionally, as in clematis, colored.

Clone One of a group of identical plants all raised from a single parent plant by vegetative propagation.

Compost Manure made of decayed vegetable matter such as kitchen waste, soft clippings, annual weeds, farmyard waste. It is incorporated in the soil to improve the soil's structure and contribute nutrients. The term is also employed to describe a rooting medium for plants, providing suitable drainage, aeration, and nutrients for maximum growth. Normally used in containers.

Conifer Any cone-bearing tree; also includes yews and junipers, which have fleshy fruits. Most conifers are evergreen, with scaly, needle-like or strap-shaped leaves.

Cordon A method of training that keeps trees, planted at an angle, to a single stem. Most frequently used for apple and pear.

Cultivar An identified strain or HYBRID that has arisen either naturally in the garden or in the wild, or by purposeful breeding and selection.

Deadheading Removing faded flowers from a plant, partly for its appearance but also to prevent it from spending its energy on producing seeds. Deadheading often produces a better crop of flowers the following year; and in some cases encourages more flowers to appear in the same year.

Deciduous Describes a plant that loses all its leaves at one time of the year, usually late autumn.

Division A method of propagation in which the crown of the plant is split into several sections, each with roots, and replanted. Normally, a method for HERBACEOUS PERENNIALS.

Double digging Digging the soil to a depth of two spits; the first with a spade, the second with a fork to break up the soil. Manure can be incorporated at the same time.

Dwarf pyramid A shape or form of apple or pear tree pruned so that the branches radiate at intervals gradually diminishing in length.

Dwarfing rootstock A ROOTSTOCK of diminished vigor, which reduces the growth of the selected scion.

Espalier A lattice-work of wood or wires on which to train trees. Also, a method of training fruit trees, by selecting lateral branches to grow horizontally on each side of the main stem.

Evergreen A plant that keeps its foliage for at least a year. A wintergreen retains its leaves for one year only.

Fastigiate Erect manner of growth in a tree or shrub, as, for example, in Irish yew.

Forcing Accelerating the growth of plants by artificial use of light or heat.

Half-hardy Describes those plants that will only survive the winter if given some kind of protection, either against a wall or under plastic sheet or glass.

Hardy Describes a plant capable of surviving for the whole of its lifespan without any protection from frost. In hot climates, hardiness may refer to a plant's resistance to drought.

Herbaceous Describes a PERENNIAL plant that dies back to the ground level each autumn or winter. The term also applies to borders that are filled largely or entirely with such plants.

Herbicide A chemical substance that kills weeds. Some act on contact (eg Roundup), others are taken in through the plant (eg Amitrole).

Hybrid A natural or man-made cross between two species or genera.

Inflorescence The part of the plant that bears the flowers.

Microclimate A climate particular to a specific situation (eg against a wall or hedge) which differs from the overall climate of the area.

Mulch A layer of decaying vegetable matter applied between plants on the surface of the soil to protect the plants from cold in the winter and from water evaporation in the summer. Mulching also helps to suppress weeds. Substances frequently used are compost, pulverized forest bark and leafmold.

Perennial A plant that lives for more than two years. Often applied exclusively to HERBACEOUS perennials.

Pinnate Describes a leaf that is composed of opposite leaflets along a central stalk.

Pollinator A second strain planted alongside the cultivated species to ensure transfer of pollen from one to another. Used most often in fruit cultivation.

Potager The French term for a vegetable garden.

Pricking out Planting out young seedlings, usually as soon as they can be handled, from the seed bed or tray into another tray, pots or the open ground.

Propagation The production of a new plant from an existing one, either sexually (by seeds) or vegetatively (eg by cuttings).

Rambler A plant, especially a rose, that has long, lax stems and is essentially droopy in habit.

Rhizome Stem that grows horizontally below ground level.

Rootstock Root or plant on which can be grafted certain species that are difficult to PROPAGATE on their own roots.

Self-clinging Describes a climber that does not require support to grow, as it attaches itself by means of short roots (ivy) or sticky, sucker-like pads (Virginia creeper).

Self-fertile Describes a plant whose ovules are fertilized by its own pollen and grow into viable seeds.

Self-seeding Describes a plant, usually an annual, that will regenerate from year to year by dispersing its seed around the garden.

Self-sterile Describes a plant whose ovules require pollen from another plant (the pollinator) to grow into viable seeds.

Semi-evergreen Describes a plant that is EVERGREEN in mild areas and DECIDUOUS in colder climes.

Shrub Any plant with many wooded stems, the main ones usually growing from the base.

Slow-release fertilizer A substance that releases the essential nutrients for the growth of a plant over a long period of time — unlike liquid fertilizer, in which the nutrients are available immediately.

Standard Any tree which has a main stem or trunk, 4 to 6 feet (1.2-1.8m) in height, with a large head at the top. The term is most commonly applied to fruit trees, ornamental topiary, roses and fuchsias.

Sub-shrub A small PERENNIAL plant with woody stem bases and soft tips, which die back every year. The term is often used to describe any small SHRUB.

Tender Describes any plant likely to be damaged by low temperatures.

Thinning Reducing the number of seedlings, branches, flowers or fruit to allow those that remain to grow with less competition, so that they achieve a greater size.

Tying in The action of securing climbers to a support, either on a wall or any other open structure. It should be done at least once a year.

Wall shrub A shrub that requires the protection and warmth of a wall to survive the winter in cooler climates.

INDEX

PICTURE CREDITS

Page numbers are followed by the photographer, and then the garden designer where applicable. The codes used are:

l left
c center
r right
t top
b bottom

Photographers
PB Paul Barker
CB Caroline Boisset
TC Tommy Candler
JG John Glover
JH Jerry Harpur
AL Andrew Lawson
SW Steven Wooster
GW George Wright

Garden designers
KA Ken Akers
HH Hillier & Hill
AK(GA) Angela Kirby (Gardening Angels)
MO Mirabel Osler
GP Gunilla Pickard

Picture Libraries
GPL The Garden Picture Library

half title:PB
title:PB
4:PB
6t,b:PB
7t,b:PB
8:PB
11tl,tr,bl,br:PB
12/13:JH
13:AL
14tl,tr,br:AL
15:AL
16:AL
18:PB
19:AL
25tl,tr,bl,br:AL
26:JH

32:PB
33:PB
39:AL
45:JH
46:PB
47:PB
48t,b:PB
49l,r:PB
51:PB
52:PB
53:JH
54:AL
56t:PB
56/57b:PB
58:PB
59:PB

60t:JH/PFC:b:AL
61:JH/HH
62:JH/MO
63:JH
64:PB
65tl,tr,bl:PB
66t:GW:b:JG
67t,b:SW/GPL
68t,b:AL
69l,r:AL
70t,b:AL
71l,r:AL
72:AL
73:TC
74/75t:AL
75bl,br:AL

76:PB
78:CB
79l,r:JH/KA
80/81:AL
82l:AL
82/83:JH
83r:AL
84:PB
86:PB
87t:JH/AK(GA):
    bl:AL:br:JH
88:AL
89l,r:AL
90:PB
92/93:PB
93tr,br:PB

94:PB
95:PB
96bl:PB
96/97:PB
97tr,br:PB
98/99:PB
100:PB
103l,tr,br:AL
104/105:PB
106l,r:JH
107:AL
108:PB
109l,c,r:PB
110/111:JH
111t:JH:b:PB
112l:JH:r:AL

113tl:PB:bl:JH:br:PB
114t:JH:b:JH/GP
115:PB
116/117:PB
118:PB
119:AL
120:AL
121:AL
122:PB
124:AL
130:AL
133:AL
134t,b:AL
135tl,tr,b:AL
136:PB
154:PB